A Think-Aloud and Talk-Aloud Approach to Building Language

Overcoming Disability, Delay, and Deficiency

D1600043

A Think-Aloud and Talk-Aloud Approach to Building Language

Overcoming Disability, Delay, and Deficiency

Reuven Feuerstein, Louis H. Falik,
Refael S. Feuerstein, & Krisztina Bohács

Foreword by Yvette Jackson

Teachers College
Columbia University
New York and London

Some of the material presented in this book appeared in Feuerstein, R., Falik, L. H., & Bohács, K. (2010). A kozvetitett szolilokvia: A nyelv es a kommunikacio mediacioja a belso beszeden keresztul (Mediated soliloquy: Mediation of language and communication through self-talk). *Magyar Pedagogia, 110*(2), 97–118, and is included by permission of the publisher.

Published by Teachers College Press, 1234 Amsterdam Avenue, New York, NY 10027

Library of Congress Cataloging-in-Publication Data

Feuerstein, Reuven, author.
   A think-aloud and talk-aloud approach to building language : overcoming
      disability, delay, and deficiency / Reuven Feuerstein, Louis H. Falik, Refael
      S. Feuerstein, & Krisztina Bohács ; foreword by Yvette Jackson.
         pages cm
   Includes bibliographical references and index.
   ISBN 978-0-8077-5393-4 (pbk. : alk. paper)
   ISBN 978-0-8077-5410-8 (hardcover : alk. paper)
      1. Children—Language. 2. Language disorders in children.
   I. Falik, Louis H., author. II. Feuerstein, Refael S., author.
   III. Bohács, Krisztina, author. IV. Title.
   LB1139.L3F48   2013
   372.6—dc23   2012035262

ISBN 978-0-8077-5393-4 (paperback)
ISBN 978-0-8077-5410-8 (hardcover)

Printed on acid-free paper
Manufactured in the United States of America

20   19   18   17   16   15   14   13   8   7   6   5   4   3   2   1

The authors wish to make a special dedication of this book,
in grateful appreciation

to

Mr. Claude Bassou

Officier de le Legion d'Honneur

Founder and President of the Feuerstein Heritage Foundation,
whose constant and heartfelt commitment and interest in our
research has made much of our work possible, as reflected in
this book and in a wide and diverse range of research activities

His hand and heart are on everything we do!

This book is dedicated to all of the children from whom we have learned and continue to be inspired by:

The children of Harlem who provided our first focus, experience, and inspiration (done under the auspices of the New York University Department of Child Development and impetus of Cynthia and Martin Deutsch):

The children, grandchildren, and great grandchildren of the authors who have anchored our thinking and provide continued opportunities to observe and practice our initiatives:

The Feuerstein Family:

Rafi and Tal Feuerstein

Betia Feuerstein Stav, Hillel, Elchanan, Michail, Chava, Achi Noam, Noga, and Avram Kaveh, Tael, Carmel Stav

Noa Feuerstein Schwartz

Avsholem and Miriam Schwartz

Aharon and Galia Feuerstein

Oria Tovah, Ruth, Matan, Daria, Ishai

Danny and Hadar Galron/Feuerstein

Naama, David, Avishai

The Falik Family:

Alan, David

Elizabeth, Rosemary, Sarah

The Bohacs Family:

Marcel

Contents

Contents

Foreword

I am unconditionally dedicated to Reuven Feuerstein. Like millions of people around the world, I have observed how he divines for and demonstrates the depth of intellectual potential of people that have been either underestimated or given up on.

I was fortunate to have discovered the work of Dr. Feuerstein while I was a teacher of students labeled as "disadvantaged minorities." I had searched for teaching strategies that would unleash and optimize the learning potential of these students in hopes of expanding the possibilities for their future—eclipsing the negative effects of debilitating conditions that so many experience and debunking the stereotypes associated with them. My search was not in vain.

Reuven Feuerstein has given us a vision of how the world can be for students who are challenged by underachievement or cognitive dysfunctions when there is belief and value in their intellectual potential and capacities. Unfortunately, in spite of knowledge of Dr. Feuerstein's work world-wide, a lack of belief in the capacities of underachieving students still persists, leaving millions of students with underdeveloped capacities and unfulfilled potential. And now, the implications of academic underachievement are even greater.

In the United States, new Common Core State Standards have caused fear that underachieving students will not be able to meet the standards and that, subsequently, their schools will be penalized. These standards extend beyond developing and refining reading skills. They reflect the need for students to be college- and career-ready, equipped with advanced levels of thinking that enable them to articulate and apply how they formulize, theorize, and hypothesize conceptual understandings so that they can be applied in innovative and productive ways for their own self-determination and the contributions they can make to society. This means that students will have to be capable of comprehending and responding to rigorous content presented through complex text across the disciplines, and apply the knowledge learned through these complex texts through a combination of higher-order cognitive skills and language-based demonstrations of understanding. Elementary schools respond to these expectations by searching for reading programs, while secondary schools add extended literacy periods. At both levels, traditional teaching will no doubt continue to be employed, resulting in a continuation of the cycle of underachievement and underdeveloped potential.

A Think-Aloud and Talk-Aloud Approach to Building Language sheds light on the most disregarded reality about underachievement in academic learning: insufficient language development. Underdeveloped language is not only the inhibitor of the cognitive processing upon which reading and academic achievement rely, it is also the barrier to articulating the vast intelligence that resides within students labeled as "low performers." This book is the oracle on accelerating and optimizing language development for those students who have lacked the experiences needed to build the critical language repertoire required for deep reading and academic achievement, and for garnering recognition for the brilliance they possess.

In *A Think-Aloud and Talk-Aloud Approach to Building Language*, Dr. Feuerstein has expounded upon the cognitive and neuroscience research reflected in his theory of Structural Cognitive Modifiability and the mediation process for transforming underachievement to high levels of learning and academic achievement to present us with another seminal process, Mediated Self-Talk (MST). MST builds on the plasticity of the brain, providing students with language and thinking models that activate neural circuits to strengthen the language development and cognitive skills required for academic learning.

The authors cogently and eloquently present us with critical understandings of the interrelationship of culture, learning, and language development through the illustrations of the models of thinking and talking-aloud inherent in Mediated Self-Talk. As students observe the modeling of language and thinking that facilitates development of learning concepts, their attention, motivation, and confidence to engage in the dialogue about these concepts are generated. This dialogue advances the development of students' language, which in turn increases their ability to construct meaning from complex, language-laden text, to articulate the meaning they have constructed with precision, and to write with clarity, coherence, and attention to detail. But as with the expectations of the Common Core State Standards, Mediated Self-Talk goes beyond the acquisition of skilled reading and writing. Mediated Self-Talk deepens reflective metacognition, increases application of higher levels of thinking (such as comparative analysis, categorical thinking, reasoning, decision-making and problem-solving), and most imperatively, arouses personal insights and confidence students can have about themselves as competent learners.

—Yvette Jackson, Ed.D.
Chief Executive Officer, National Urban Alliance for Effective Education

Preface

This book presents the reader with a new approach to stimulating and enriching language development in young children, and those older children and adults who present delays or deficiency in function. It is based on the application of self-talk flowing from inner thoughts that are communicated aloud to the listener. We have labeled this process as a *soliloquy* to convey its unique quality of expression as a natural occurrence in human thinking and interaction—the talking to oneself that we humans do in moments of self-discovery or contemplation, or times of stress or personal conflict. It is what Shakespeare's Hamlet does after he discovers his mother's and uncle's calumny. Throughout this book we will use the term *soliloquy* as a shorthand for describing complex but important aspects of the process. Our goal is to turn this natural tendency to the direction of helping our children to develop their language and thinking, and formulate what we call in this book *mediated self-talk* (MST). Thus, we will use MST and *soliloquy* interchangeably to describe the same process. The theory and resulting methodology are based on the theory of structural cognitive modifiability (SCM) and the practices of mediated learning experience (MLE), and are applied within a variety of clinical and educational modalities. The approach and related methodology are supported by contemporary developments in the brain sciences, namely the discovery and description of the mirror neurons leading to the human potential for neural plasticity.

In this book we develop and describe the potential of MST, provided through the application of MLE, to create both immediate learning and social development, acting through the promotion of neural plasticity, as the catalyst to consolidate and transcend language acquisition and proficiency into needed conceptual and cognitive development. The reader is offered a description of the theory, conceptual development, and then a number of practical suggestions to implement the method. In this sense, the volume is designed to be a guidebook for potential interventions.

We do not view ourselves as language specialists. We have drawn on well-accepted research and accepted thinking regarding the structure and development of language, and added to it our ideas for bringing MLE into an active relationship with the goals (both developmental and structural) of linguistic functioning. Obviously, we see a close correspondence between language development and cognitive processes, and a needed integration if children and others will be able to achieve their cognitive potential. Throughout our discussions, we seek to integrate the theory (SCM) and the practices (MLE), and suggest innovative ways of bringing modifying experiences to the children and others in need.

The reader may well view the methods and intentions of MST as appropriate for all developing children, and applicable in the normal life experience of children. We believe that this is an important aspect of development, and it should be actively promoted, for the well-being of children and their families, and to provide a platform for academic, social, and eventual life development. We thus focus our presentation in two directions—that of the normal developmental processes of language acquisition and thinking, and toward those children and adults who experience—for a variety of reasons—language delay, deficiency, or loss of functions. Both needs require, and will benefit from, an intentional and systematic application of the method. As such, we are writing for parents, teachers, and care providers (including the "non-professional") who are in a position to provide an enriched verbal experience for their children and students. We are also writing for the professional—speech and language specialists; therapists working from the vocational, occupational, or social/developmental perspectives—for whom the addition of language development and stimulation methods will add important tools to their treatment repertoires.

At a certain point in the book, we address the natural settings in which MST is offered, as well as the resistances that many parents, caretakers, and adults may experience in attempting to utilize and sustain the method. We have found that it is often difficult for the MST provider to talk to the child when he or she does not respond, and to bring the structural elements of language into the daily verbal "interactions" with the recipient of the soliloquy. For these reasons, this book emphasizes the need and provides information to those who would use MST to structure the linguistic production and sustain it—in the face of lack of response and potential frustration.

The book thus responds to several needs and perspectives. It presents the theory, concepts, and research that serve as the foundation and support for the approach. It then moves to the provision of practical applications. While we have striven to write in an accessible way, minimizing technical terminology and jargon, there is an inevitable need to elucidate concepts and present terms of a certain degree of complexity. We hope that the reader will bear with us, understand the need to master aspects of complex processes, and allow our illustrations and examples to clarify what may be initially abstract or confusing.

We do not develop this material in isolation. In its earliest formation, in the 1960s, the senior author benefited from the friendship and collaboration of a group of scholars who shared his concern for the issues presented in this book. They accepted his theoretical and methodological innovations and helped to develop and further shape the work. Among them were Professors Alfred Friedman, Cynthia and Martin Deutsch, Abraham Tannenbaum, Harry Passow, Milton Schwebel, and Martin Hamberger, who provided support, inspiration, and technical suggestions in the early phases of the work. We are blessed with many very competent professionals and experts, from all over the world, who have studied our theories and are implementing SCM and MLE in diverse and innovative ways. Our Malaysian colleagues Foo Siang Mun and Soo Kui Chian have adapted MST for children within the autistic spectrum and those with long-standing language delays, starting with very early versions of the method and extending it to academic skill development and the overcoming of emotional and social dysfunction. Several of the cases in Chapter 10 are drawn from their innovative work.

At the Feuerstein Institute (formerly known as the International Center for the Enhancement of Learning Potential [ICELP]) in Jerusalem, we have a team of dedicated specialists working with children and adults who have helped us to develop and refine the approach as it is described in this book. Those who have made a contribution to this book are our speech and language therapists, coordinated by Rina Frei Schreiber, including Simha Dray, Dara Rogoff, Revital Rubin, and Haguit Szpeker; those working with brain-injured individuals under the coordination of Idit Dorfzaun-Harif, including Shira Ettinger, Tehila Ganor, and Hadar Tvito; and providers of occupational therapy and inclusion programs for young children, under the direction of Chana Nakav and Chaya Ginton respectively. All of these individuals have tried out various aspects of the program and made valuable suggestions for improvements and applications.

We also want to acknowledge the role that our editor, Jean Ward, has played in the development of not only this book, but as an advocate and supporter of our work. We know that she has a team of talented colleagues contributing to this project, but her insight into the relevance of the potential for cognitive modifiability and mediated learning experience, and its potential to change the learning and lives of humanity, confirm and inspire us.

In Chapter 1 we define the concept of MST and differentiate it from other early language approaches. We place the method in the context of where, when, why, and with whom it can be utilized. Chapter 2 presents its early development; what conditions and issues stimulated Professor

Feuerstein, the senior author, to formulate and implement it; and its relationship to mediated learning experience that serves as its primary mechanism of transmission. Chapter 3 brings the scientific support for the method to the reader, emphasizing the role of mirror neurons and findings from the "new" neurosciences. These chapters can be considered as the first part of the book.

Chapters 4, 5, and 6 offer the reader specific and somewhat technical information on language development and practical applications. In these chapters we provide a number of suggestions and specific formulations of language interactions that can be adapted for the needs and circumstances of the children (and others). These three chapters taken together would be sufficient preparation for a parent, teacher, or other professional to begin to use the soliloquy process to help children in their care.

The remaining chapters discuss aspects of applications, particularly those directed toward "going beyond" the soliloquy, and adapting it to the developing needs and changes observed in those to whom it has been applied. Chapter 7 describes the child's self-talk—as differentiated from the adult's soliloquy. Chapter 8 relates MST to various formally diagnosed and described language disorders. Chapters 9 and 10 present case illustrations of the application of MST to a variety of developmental and behavioral needs. And Chapter 11 summarizes the state of the approach, and concludes by reviewing critical aspects of the approach that require clear differentiation and understanding of potential outcomes and needs for the future. The Appendix raises some issues for further study.

Our initial experiences with earlier, experimental versions of MST have made us very optimistic about its potential for helping in both developmental and therapeutic applications. The results reported by those who have used it are strikingly positive, so much so that we have been reluctant to pass on many of the more unusual findings. This includes children with long-standing language dysfunctions, involving delays, lack of expressive language, and behavioral problems affecting language, like autistic spectrum disorders, depression, social acting out, and the like. There is evidence that MST, provided in a systematic and competent way, leads to the stimulation and production of language in those who have not talked for long periods of time. We give you a picture of some of these changes in Chapters 9 and 10, but remain cautious about some of the more surprising changes that have been reported.

Nevertheless, we think that this book will open you to a very promising and needed implementation of mediated learning experience directed to language acquisition and development, and we hope that you and the children and adults about whom you are concerned will benefit from it.

CHAPTER 1

Mediating Language Development

Talking and Thinking Aloud to Overcome Language Poverty, Delay, and Disability

This book introduces the reader to an innovative approach to stimulating language development in children whose speech is in need of systematic stimulation or whose speech development has been delayed or impaired. Throughout we will be addressing two sets of readers: parents and caretakers who interact with their children on a daily basis, and educators and other professionals concerned with improving speech and language. Both groups can benefit from the approach we describe, and can in fact collaborate with one another to respond to the needs of children. Our approach is directed toward all of these populations who work with children (or with adults of whatever age) who can benefit from a systematic, mediated exposure to language. However, the approach described in this book is particularly valuable to those who are at risk of failing to develop linguistic processes due to a variety of conditions—autism, brain injury, genetic/chromosomal conditions, language poverty, language deterioration or loss due to aging, and other kinds of developmental delays. Our approach is innovative because it applies our concept of mediated learning experience (as we describe in Chapter 2) to what is now known about how the brain functions, and that can be modified by exposure to language. For younger children it provides an early and intensive intervention, providing a greater, more available, and systematically planned and executed exposure to language.

The approach seems simple, and many will say that they already do it! In fact, it should be a part of our natural interaction with our children. However, under certain important conditions, it requires an understanding of processes and application of skills that, while not difficult to achieve, require a particular perspective and body of knowledge, and a conscious and purposeful awareness, that often make it far from simple to initiate and sustain.

What are we talking about? We believe that natural self-talk occurs within every thinking individual and is an important resource for the stimulation of language awareness and acquisition. For the child, the adult's self-talk reflects what is being experienced, helps in planning and interpreting, and links direct exposure with the "indirect" input of language, symbolism, and deeper levels of meaning. We call this *soliloquy*—to describe the speech of a person speaking alone or appearing to speak only to oneself (think of Shakespeare's Hamlet or Lady Macbeth—*"To be or not to be, that is the question . . ."* or *"Out, out damned spot . . ."*). For us, soliloquy describes the adult who engages in self-talk, in the presence of the child, while expecting only that the child *overhears* the language produced, and is not required to attend, respond, or even acknowledge that listening is occurring. This experience (for the one who "overhears") creates important changes that take place in the brain (see Chapter 3), and a platform for both cognitive and language development.

We further define the intentional, systematic, and planned use of this approach as *mediated self-talk* (MST), to convey the intimate relationship between the soliloquy (self-talk) and the application of mediated learning experience (MLE). You will see MST and MLE referred to often in this book, as we elaborate on the concepts and describe their important contribution to the process of language acquisition and development.

It is important to understand why this approach was formulated (the theory) and when and for what reasons it was formulated (the historical context). It is based on what senior author Professor Reuven Feuerstein observed, and how his observations fit into the context of the times and the needs of the children and families with whom he met and worked. The theory guides us to an understanding of the potential for modifying the learning and behavior of children, and how this modifiability goes well beyond behavior and affects the cognitive and neurological structures of the individual. It links the role and function of language to the process of cognitive development. With these two perspectives in mind—the potential for modifiability and the role of language—one has options to effect meaningful change when one encounters children whose life experiences prevent their development (due to poverty; being members of culturally different communities where the first language may be rich but the language of the dominant culture limited; or having a developmental, genetic, or chromosomal condition).

The options are positive and accessible. Research neurophysiology has made it clear that using MST as an early and natural intervention—either as a developmental experience or targeted toward specific developmental or functional deficits—can enhance and develop cognition and learning through the medium of linguistic formulation and interaction.

The chapters that follow are written for both parents and caregivers who may not have a background in language development, education, or psychology, but are also appropriate for educators and specialists who may wish to adopt the practices in their own work or help parents and others undertake them. Our intention is to be accessible and informative, but also to offer sufficient technical information so that MST will be well grounded, specific, and functional. We will provide both the theoretical and conceptual rationale and a practical guide that will lead toward the effective use of the approach.

MST can be applied by parents, teachers, and other caregivers who interact with children and other learners who are at risk at early ages and stages of development, or at later periods in situations of language delay or loss. If one understands the *what, why,* and *how* of such activities, one will be able to focus and direct them toward facilitating important aspects of language development, and sustain the activity in the face of what appears to be lack of response, progress, etc.—as we shall discuss in several other places in this book.

WHAT IS "MEDIATED SELF-TALK" (MST)?

What is MST, and what it is not? There are many ways of describing and interacting with the child to enhance language development. MST presents particular qualities that are reflected in its practice, making a unique contribution to the neurophysiological development of the brain. In Chapter 3 we will discuss this in detail.

MST describes the process of constructing and implementing actions that mediate language awareness, acquisition, and development. In later chapters we will describe how to construct and implement it, what to observe in the individual to whom it is directed, and how to adapt it to the readiness, needs, and responses of the learner.

MST is an intentional act that is undertaken by an adult (parent, teacher, or caretaker) and directed toward a child. It is the act of the adult verbalizing—within the hearing of the child—but without the expectation (or linguistic construction requiring) that the child will or should respond—thus being a *soliloquy*. When the child engages in self-talk this can also be characterized as soliloquy, with many of the same qualities, functional objectives, and response/interaction potentials. The verbalization is designed to be overheard but not responded to. This is the *sine qua non* of MST. If the soliloquy is dependent on the "listener" responding, there will be the risk that the producer will limit or stop producing the rich linguistic environment—that he or she will stop talking to the child. Thus, sustaining the soliloquy is often very difficult for adults to maintain in the face of the child's manifest inattention. Adults must be encouraged to persist even though the situation feels asocial and may be unsatisfying (for the adult). If we are not responded to, we usually become unwilling to keep talking. This is an important issue—we will return to it later.

MST has several "built-in" necessary attributes:

- it is usually and initially related to concurrent activities that the child observes, experiences, and remembers;
- it contains adult forms of grammar and syntax that the child hears, assimilates, and later imitates;
- it brings in missing elements in the child's linguistic repertoire;
- it has qualities of embellishment, exaggeration, and repetition that stimulate attending; and
- it orients the listener to elements of past and future.

Each of these will be described in later chapters. The adult's soliloquy exposes the child to speech in a very intentional (goal-oriented, systematic, highly focused, etc.) manner—directed initially toward language stimulation, and later extended to aspects where functional or developmental deficiencies have been observed and identified.

MST incorporates three major components of mediated learning experience (MLE). The soliloquy is constructed and conveyed in a way that brings elements of intentionality, the mediation of transcendence, and the mediation of meaning to the interaction. Each of these parameters will be described Chapter 2.

Children naturally engage in soliloquy. It is also a form of self-talk. It rehearses and practices linguistic formulations of experiences that allow the child to experiment, self-reflect, and enrich his or her interaction with the environment—making early social and cognitive connections. This is a natural outcome of the child's linguistic development, and is related to what is overheard and experienced; here, too—at least in the earlier stages—the adult's role is to listen and respond in very limited ways (gently, and conveying that the child is being listened to).

For those with special needs, where delays or deficits interfere with language acquisition or proficiency (such as apraxia, brain injury, physical disabilities, environmental deprivation, genetic/chromosomal conditions, deterioration, or loss due to aging, autistic spectrum disorders, etc.), MST can be used to help overcome deficits, stimulate growth, and bring the learner into more normal social contact and communication with the world. To reiterate: The interaction is MST when it embodies

1. systematic activities,
2. a knowledge of the processes of language development, and
3. aspects of language awareness and acquisition.

Functioning can be enhanced, gaps in development can be addressed, and opportunities to advance cognitive development can be facilitated. For both children and adults manifesting different forms and etiologies of language deficit, MST can be a vital approach to overcome these deficits and provide foundations for improved functioning.

MST also contains various "paralinguistic" elements that enhance its effect. Gestures, exaggerated intonation, variations in rhythm, facial mimicry, and other elements are added to the verbalization in order to prepare the child to receive and understand the meaning of the communication and deepen the experience. These will be described in Chapter 6.

LANGUAGE STIMULATION AND DEVELOPMENT THROUGH MST

Researchers have described the rapidity with which children acquire linguistic formulations in response to experience, how their vocabularies increase, and how they practice and master syntactic structures (Kuhl, 2004; Kuhl & Meltzoff, 1982). In this section we will describe several critical elements of early language stimulation and acquisition, and discuss the ways in which they are similar and contributory to MST and how they should be differentiated.

Motherese

The way that adults often talk to infants and very young children has been called *motherese* (Fernald & Kuhl, 1987; Lieven, 1994). Research has shown that motherese is part of a general tendency to modify infant-directed interactions. It has been shown that adults also modify their body motions—characterized by exaggerated movements and repetitions, a kind of "motionese" that correlates with the verbal components. The adult responds to the infant's or young child's early "pre-language" verbal utterances and linguistic formulations. Motherese uses shortened and simplified syllables in words, heightened pitch, exaggerated intonation, and increased repetition of words and clauses—often imitating the child's articulatory production and prosody. There is evidence that infants do benefit from this type of linguistic interaction—enhancing attention and promoting processes of speech (Lieven, 1994). But MST differs from motherese in significant ways. In Table 1.1 we compare motherese to MST.

Table 1.1. Comparing Motherese to MST

Motherese	Mediated Self-Talk (MST)
shortened and simplified words	higher level (in complexity and vocabulary) than the child's language—the child will talk like this 10 years later; not currently present in the child's linguistic repertoire
non-mediated	mediated
natural and unconscious	means effort: the parents have to do it without really wanting it
Examples of Motherese vocabulary:	Example of Mediated Self-Talk:
beddy-bye (go to bed, sleeping, bedtime) binkie (pacifier or blanket) blankie (blanket) boo-boo (wound or bruise)	I am looking at this *ladybug. Lady'bug. La'dybug.* I touch it with my hands—I put it on my palms. The *ladybug* is *crawling* on my palm, like you can crawl.
not consciously *mediated*	*Mediated:* Our intention is to willfully present the child a language that is far above what he or she already knows. We hope to establish verbal reciprocity one day—but until then we have to wait. Surely the mirror neurons of the child "reciprocate" our intentions. In MLE, reciprocity doesn't have to stand by itself. Without reciprocity, an interaction containing intentionality and mediation of meaning and transcendence can still be MLE. By declaring (enunciating) an act, my soliloquy is filled with meaning, as I am showing how the action is done.

The language of MST is not simplified in vocabulary, articulation, grammar, or syntax. It is *adult language* in form and structure. It may have elements of motherese—particularly those of exaggerated intonation or prosody, emphasis, and repetition. These elements are included to engage (but not require) the attention of the child. The language of MST is expressly produced for the child to *overhear* formal and complex forms of speech, with the intention that they will be assimilated in the child's awareness and eventually imitated. There are important consequences for the cognitive structures and neurological development of this exposure, as we will elaborate on in Chapter 3 and elsewhere in this book.

Overhearing

Overheard language has been identified as a major component in the acquisition of speech and the development of linguistic elements—vocabulary, syntactical structures, rhythms (accents), social interactions linked to language, and the like (Kuhl, 2004). A number of researchers have identified how very young children, those on the verge of moving from "preverbal to verbal," use words that they were not "taught," but that they were simply exposed to by listening to the language of others. These children acquire constructions that they have heard, and put together linguistic formulations of great complexity. Children as young as 12 weeks imitate overheard words (Kuhl & Melzhoff, 1996). Vocal expressions are copied at 18 weeks of age (Bloom, Hood, & Lichtbown, 1974). Vocabulary expansion has been observed in children described as "more imitative" at 13 months, leading to larger vocabularies 4 months later (Masur, 1997).

In MST the child overhears what is spoken, with the linguistic constructions contained in the soliloquy produced to relate to specifically identified needs of the child being exposed to it. The soliloquy does not limit children to the language with which he or she is already familiar, but exposes the child to more advanced forms and vocabulary. *Overhearing* becomes a primary mechanism of MST. However, while MST assumes that the language will be overheard, it differs from overheard speech in that it does not occur randomly. Rather, there is a clear and structured awareness on the part of the adult that the child be exposed to an intentionally selected content and structure. Overhearing appears to have a significant effect on activating the mirror neurons and contributing to neural plasticity, thus giving the soliloquy an important neurological development function, in addition to its other benefits for language and social communication development (see Chapter 3).

Both motherese and overheard speech have been researched, and their contributions to language development and social communication in normally developing children have been described (e.g., Au, Knightly, Jun, & Oh, 2002; Ohima-Takane, Goodz, & Derevensky, 2008).

Imitation

Children imitate language early, rapidly, and relatively automatically (Indefrey & Levelt, 2004). However, many delays in speech acquisition have to do with difficulties in imitation due to apraxia or lack of focusing (see Chapter 9). Moreover, there is now strong evidence from direct observations of cortical functions that imitative processes are facilitated by mirror neurons that are part of neural resonance circuits in the brain (Siegel, 2007), and that language exposure and learning are important early facilitators (Skoyles, 2008, 2010). There is further research signifying that early linguistic experience stimulates the development of cognitive processes. And by *early* we mean in infancy, within the first weeks of life, even before there are any overt indications of focusing, awareness, or articulatory responsiveness. There is general agreement in the field of language development that imitation is a central aspect of acquisition, and that the processes of imitation continue throughout the life of the learner. The young child acquires speech in large part through mimicry of the spoken word.

Circular Reactions

This concept, formulated by Piaget (1977; Piaget & Inhelder, 1969), explains much of what we have just described above. Piaget's description of *circular reactions*—elaborating some of Baldwin's early (1885) conceptual formulations—suggested that, cognitively, children are influenced by the repetition of their actions (with some variations) in response to environmental stimuli. This is viewed as occurring very early in life, within the first few months, as the infant observes and reacts to novel and complex stimuli. Piaget considered that this early experience laid the foundation for the later bringing of stimuli and responses into both awareness and a responsive repertoire (processes he labeled as *assimilation* and *accommodation*). It is our view that language plays a key role in this experience, as the child is being talked to, is listening to the surrounding language, and is beginning to respond. Those around the child respond to the response and create a kind of linguistic circular reaction. One often observes an infant dropping something, an adult picking it up and giving it back, and the infant repeating the action to generate a similar response from the adult. Soliloquy thus provides early, systematic, contextual, and repeated stimuli to instigate the process of language stimulation and awareness.

Private Speech

Private speech is a concept that originated in the work of Russian cognitive psychologist Lev Vygotsky (1987). It describes children's use of language to plan and organize their behavior. Diaz and colleagues (Diaz & Berk, 1992; Diaz, Winsler, Atencio, & Harbers, 1992) show how children use private speech to internalize the meaning of adult speech, enabling them to move from socially meaningful interactions to cognitive understanding

(Diaz, Neal, & Amaya-Williams, 1992). When children engage in soliloquy, they are vocalizing their private speech processes. When we discuss self-talk in the child (see Chapter 7), we will address how the child uses language as an external manifestation of the important internal processes of reflecting upon experiences, self-planning, and understanding that which is (or has been) experienced. We also show how this develops in the child in the extensive case study presented in Chapter 9.

WHERE TO APPLY MST:
IN EVERYDAY LIFE, IN SCHOOL, AND IN THERAPY

Typically, MST occurs in everyday life, in familiar and natural social environments. In this context it has a high potential for repetition, and is provided by adults who are familiar and intimate in the life of the child. But because MST is a very useful tool for children and others who experience language deficits or delays, it has a significant potential contribution in speech and language therapy. When MST is used in this modality of treatment, it differs in duration and exposure from its use in the normal, everyday encounters between children and adults.

For those with special needs, the therapeutic objectives will be similar to those for the general provision of MST—the improvement of language acquisition and structure by providing models and practice. Important differences have to do with the structure of the exposure: Contact in remedial interventions is typically limited to 1 or 2 hours per week, usually in an isolated, clinical environment. In the therapeutic context, MST can be provided by trained clinicians who presumably have considerable knowledge about the processes of speech and language development and choose to add MST to their repertoire of therapeutic tools. They are able to observe, plan, and adjust the MST to meet therapeutic goals. But the therapeutic application of MST does not preclude its use in normal, everyday activities. In fact, under certain circumstances the therapeutic contact can enhance it by modeling for parents how to do it and providing support for parents as they apply it.

An important bridge from therapeutic to daily life applications occurs when the therapist trains the parent or caretaker in the application of MST, and then provides encouragement, support, consultation on applications, and the like. (Several cases presented in Chapter 10 illustrate this well.)

The elements that we have described above make important contributions to language acquisition and development. MST contains some similar elements and some important differences. Both overhearing and imitation are present in MST. We consider overhearing to be a critical mechanism in the process of MST. Imitation is also an important element, but is somewhat delayed, given the structuring of the soliloquy so as not to expect or produce overt responses on the part of the child. Later, after the learner has overheard and assimilated the content of the MST, in different contexts and with repetition, imitation certainly plays a part. In our view, imitation and overhearing are functions of the same phenomena that are facilitated by the actions of the mirror neurons and neurophysiological processes (we further elaborate on this in Chapter 3).

To summarize, soliloquy in MST presents the learner with language models (incorporating elements of articulation, semantics, syntax, and pragmatic meaning—see Chapters 3 and 5) that are overheard, assimilated, and processed in the neural imaging circuits, "made ready" for later imitation, and made possible by the development of the articulatory capacity of the child. Both are related to the eventual (but relatively rapid) vocabulary and semantic/syntactical learning expansion that characterizes language acquisition in normally developing young children (Kuhl & Meltzoff, 1982; Skoyles, 2010). However, this may not occur spontaneously in development, and may benefit from the systematically imposed exposure of the child to the qualities of verbal/linguistic structure and production that are the essential elements of MST.

TO WHOM SHOULD MST BE DIRECTED?

MST is an appropriate approach for the developing young child and for children or older individuals (children or adults) who show language delays. Therapeutically it can be used with individuals of any age who have experienced loss of speech due to brain trauma, or due to other conditions (such as aging, lack of stimulation, etc.) that affect language functions. Thus, in the application of the approach, the main focus should be on the needs for and potential to apply MST in a systematic and intentional manner to address language development, often in conjunction with other interventions.

WHY DO IT?

Self-talk is a very natural aspect of thinking and is thus accessible for both adults and children. Almost from the beginning, humans begin to self-vocalize as they acquire linguistic models to describe their experience. In Chapter 5 we describe how infants and young children become very aware and start to imitate what they hear (and what they experience in relation to the linguistic models that they are exposed to). The MLE that becomes a central component of MST is directed toward bringing to the interaction elements of language development and the learner's awareness that are observed and assessed as needed in the learner's development. In this way MST becomes a meaningful tool in the repertoire of interventions with these populations.

WHO CAN AND SHOULD DO IT?

MST is primarily designed to be undertaken by parents, and the primary family system of the child, to enhance the quality of the language experience. This is described in the case study presented in Chapter 9. It can be used by teachers of children with speech delays, in the classroom, as well as with children individually or in groups who come from limited linguistic environments, or a different original language from that of the school. In Chapter 6 we describe the natural occurrences in the child's and family's life that are rich opportunities to apply MST, and point out how the qualities of MST are often spontaneously present in adult/child interactions. The natural environment can be used systematically to provide MST. Encouragement, focus, training, and ongoing support are necessary to sustain and develop MST in such situations. This is because, as we describe above, there is a strong tendency to experience discouragement and consequent resistance to continuing on the part of the adult or teacher: If the child is not responding, the experience of the adult is "asocial" and unrewarding, it feels as though one is "talking to the wall," or "talking to oneself," or the adult may feel that "people who talk to themselves are crazy." We return to this very important source of inhibition in Chapter 6.

Additionally, we believe that effective use of MST requires knowledge of the structural aspects of language development, and how to understand and employ the parameters of MLE. Both of these dimensions will be discussed at several places in subsequent chapters.

WHEN SHOULD IT BE DONE?

MST can be applied very early in the life of the child—well before the child can respond linguistically, even before one observes the child attending to speech. There is much evidence that the sublinguistic aspects of speech (rhythm, tonality, facial expression) are perceived by the infant, and that they contribute to attaching meaning to the words that accompany the non-verbal elements of the communication.

MST should be done repetitively and consistently by different individuals in the child's life. A rule of thumb: The greater the need, or the more focused the deficit, the more structured input and repetition should be provided. However, repetition alone is not enough. An operational principle of MLE is to provide repetition with variation—doing things again, using the same rule or relationship, but varying some aspect of the stimulation. This provides novelty that keeps attention focused and permits transcendence and generalization (see Chapter 2). We do not say the same thing the same way every time, but we use a different cadence, different relevant examples, and the like.

WHAT ARE THE APPROPRIATE APPLICATIONS?

MST is a potentially powerful way to overcome many of the communication difficulties experienced by children and adults. There is often a *poverty of language* in many populations, for a variety of reasons. For the developing child, this linguistic and/or communication deficit limits a whole range of cognitive and social developments. For the school-aged child, especially those who have not received rich oral language exposure, communication difficulties become a crucial factor in low or deficient functioning in the acquisition of the academic skills necessary for adequate or enhanced performance.

A word of caution is necessary here. The applications of MST are relatively new and limited data regarding effectiveness have been generated. We are optimistic, but recognize that there yet is a lot to learn and discover.

We can summarize the use of MST applied to several kinds of needs:

1. to *enhance the acquisition* of language in young children who show limited linguistic development,
2. to *provide extra or intensive stimulation* for individuals who are at risk of not developing language adequacy or proficiency,
3. to *overcome already manifested deficits* in communication, and
4. to use language processes to *improve socialization and affective connections* in situations where they are deficient or blocked.

A potentially interesting application of several of these variables can be considered with Alzheimer's patients or with those on the geriatric spectrum to prevent deterioration or restore lost language.

CREATING CONDITIONS FOR SOLILOQUY

Soliloquy (MST) presents an experience that is at the same time both natural and unique. As a process, it is a natural part of the child's experience in an environment of talking, thinking, describing, and understanding. Soliloquy creates a particular linguistic environment. It brings a systematic and purposeful perspective to the interaction, to achieve desired and needed goals. What then are the conditions, and our reasons for developing them? We follow Piaget in holding that to a large extent language precedes thought: *first you speak and then you think*. The phenomenon of sublingual speech, where articulatory muscles (in the throat) are activated during mental activities (when no speech is evidenced), is an example.

Exposure of the child, or any individual with language deficiency or delay, to a rich and immediately available linguistic environment plays an important role in determining the acquisition of both language and the conceptual processes stimulated by it. There is a direct relationship.

The Role of Attention

MST is a process of "self-talk." The place of attention is differently conceived, however. The goal is to stimulate awareness and then put into linguistic form what is observed and overheard in the environment of the child, thereby developing in the child what language specialists refer to as *receptive language*. The self-talk of MST, or what we label the "soliloquy," links internal, receptive knowledge as an early component in the development of expressive language. Thus it has the potential to enrich the child's ideational and conceptual processes, extending to cognitive awareness and social/emotional behaviors. These ideational processes precede and then support the receptive and expressive phases of language, and bridge them to wider and developing experiences.

The Expectation of a Response

If verbalization is directed toward children with the expectation that they will respond, there may be disappointment. When they do not respond, this may close down the interaction—"*If they are not responding, they are not paying attention, and I am wasting my time!*" However, many children at young ages, and some older children, are *unidirectional*—they do not speak while they are listening (engaging in the process of *overhearing*). This may be due to the problem of simultaneously needing to deal with input (listening to what is being said or paying attention to actions observed) and plan the output (thinking about what will be said or done behaviorally). For such individuals the communicator should slow speech models and allow for exaggerated response time. One should look for subtle indications of responding that are non-verbal—tilting of the head, orientation of the body, the slowing down of motor behaviors, and the like.

But for the child who does not respond—the adult speaks and they do not—the adult should not stop the soliloquy. If the speech of the adult is *conditioned* by the expectation of receiving a response, and if the child does not talk, the adult should not stop or reduce verbal interactions with the child. The provision of the verbal language should not depend on how much attention the child gives, or how much response is given at the moment of the utterances. To the contrary, MST is a modality of acting independently of the attention of the child or his or her response. Additionally, MST is strengthened when the parent or other mediator accompanies their soliloquy behavior with an intentional and systematically planned enunciation of their actions, accompanied by appropriate gesticulation and demonstration of the enunciated actions, and is reflective of their observations of the child's behavior, their feelings, or other aspects of their reactions. All of these will be described, illustrated, and discussed in the chapters that follow.

MST as a Model of Activity

Because soliloquy *models* an activity as it is happening, it enriches and elaborates on direct experience, provides focusing behavior, and creates conditions of interest, potential engagement, and eventual response. For example:

> *We are crossing the street. I look in both directions. I see if cars are coming. I see that it is safe. I step out into the street. I look both ways to be sure that it is safe to cross, etc. I hold your hand so that we can cross the street safely. I look both ways for cars that may be coming.*

This elaboration of and focus on a direct experience can be considered one of the main dynamics that explains why the soliloquy activity is paid attention to, even though the talk is not explicitly directed toward the child or demanding his or her attention.

We will describe in Chapter 3 how this is understood and supported by the mechanism of the mirroring phenomenon in the brain, integrating the language, motor, and ideational levels of responsiveness, and bringing about in the non-speaking child a neurologically related "linguistic" activity. It is now neurophysiologically clear that soliloquy stimulates neural activity. We further hold, consistent with the neurological effects, that the activity enriches the repertoire of knowledge, widening the range of observations, and laying a foundation for interactions and insights.

What Are the Functional Elements of MST?

The key elements are the non-demand quality of the interaction, the relevance of language to what is being experienced, the structural quality of the language, the repetition, and the embellishment and exaggeration (along with gestures).

Returning again to neurophysiology in the processes of language acquisition, the firing of the mirror neurons observing an act upon an object (in this case both the activity and accompanying linguistic production) may be triggered by listening to the "noise" that the act produces. The noise is the "language" that first accompanies and then substitutes for the act. At the outset, the child needs to observe the action on the object, but eventually the language that accompanies the act allows/produces the same mental activation (firing of the neurons) as the act itself—contributing significantly to cognitive and neural development. There is much scientific evidence for this. We review it in Chapter 3.

The processes of language development, as well as the structural, social/interactional, and cognitive elements, are critical components in the provision of MST, and will be addressed in more detail in the following chapters.

CHAPTER 2

Theoretical Foundations for Mediated Self-Talk (MST)

ANTECEDENTS TO THE DEVELOPMENT OF THE THEORY OF SOLILOQUY

Children learn speech models as they observe and listen to the verbal interactions around them, first as a passive experience and gradually experimenting with and imitating what they hear. Initially, early expressive language can be considered a form of deferred imitation. Imitation does not solely occur in response to sensorially experienced perception; it is also a consequence of internalized models that are potentially expressed imitatively—divorced from direct contact with the model. The neurophysiological basis for speech acquisition suggests that the mechanism of mirror neurons (discussed in detail in Chapter 3) is an important source of language acquisition.

But how does this occur? What are its mechanics, dynamics, and sensitivities? The senior author has been contemplating these questions for some time. He began to consider the formulation of concepts and techniques to improve the language functioning in populations of children at risk as early as 1963. He began with a consideration of the succession of events leading to the acquisition of speech, both receptive and expressive, and the mastery of expressive aspects of enunciation, words, and sentences. Many educators and specialists in speech and language development agreed that there was a need to intervene intensively to help children—particularly those from minority groups where their primary language exposure was not the standard mode of expression in the larger culture in which they functioned, especially in school. The objective was to find ways to enrich the linguistic environments of these children, in order to create a modality of communication leading to more adequate acquisition of the skills required in educational and other settings.

One such approach considered at the time was the construction of *responsive environments* to elicit speech. Various innovative and engaging devices were developed: a small train that climbed a mountain as long as the child was speaking, a clown whose nose lit up when it was being spoken to, and a telephone that children would use to talk to their parents or other communicators. Children were put in front of these "toys," and encouraged to use them to generate spontaneous language. The spontaneity was encouraged by the fact that the clown did not react if the child was not talking. On the telephone, the parents "at the other end of the line" were instructed to interact with their children in a meaningful way to show the child that they were listening, and respond accordingly. The parents, however, in this situation were observed not to respond to their child's speech utterances other than make non-meaningful sounds ("uh huhs," etc.). As Professor Feuerstein observed these interactions, it appeared to him that what was being elicited and reinforced was the language that already existed in the child's repertoire, that there was no enrichment provided by any of these devices or the adults' use of them, and often the children simply made unintelligible sounds.

He concluded that children from culturally different, minority populations needed to be encouraged to talk, but that these devices did not address the structuring of the content or quality of the speech. More was needed than simply an emphasis on increasing the verbal output of the child. He first experimented by posing questions as a way to enrich the vocabulary of the children. This led to an early variant of mediated soliloquy, and the search to find ways to communicate and encourage responses in a systematic way.

Another aspect of the needed communication process was identified. Feuerstein observed that many people in the targeted populations, as well as their teachers and caretakers, spoke to children in childish ways that were *presumed* to foster understanding (the motherese we described in Chapter 1). He concluded that this actually impoverished the child's linguistic environment. He observed that even in this restricted linguistic interaction, if the children did not respond, the adults in their environments stopped speaking to them.

Professor Feuerstein then expanded the process to encourage caregivers (parents, teachers, etc.) not to limit their speech only to questions, and when questioning not to stop questioning if the child did not respond. Rather, they should generate a rich linguistic environment *even if* the child did not respond or appear to be focused. He proposed to a group of teachers of kindergarten children in an inner-city environment of the United States that they consider using this approach. It was presented as a modality of exposing linguistic stimuli to children—*whether or not the children appeared to see or hear what was being enunciated and portrayed*, and *not limited to those parts of the language that were presumed to be understood*. At first this was resisted, as it appeared contrary to the generally accepted view that the normal developmental progression of speech required a level of socialization *before* such communication was deemed meaningful, and because it seemed akin to what was considered pathological speech. A typical comment from those who resisted was, "Do you really want children exposed to models of *people talking to themselves*?"

At this time, the concepts of the socio-linguist Basel Bernstein (1959) were becoming known. The 1960s in the United States were a time of awakening to the educational and social service needs of inner-city, poor, and minority populations. One of the consequences was the initiation of the Head Start program, and a widened focus on educational, social, academic, and linguistic factors in development. Feuerstein thought about Bernstein's concept of "public language," referring to the restricted language (of the child) that often did not refer to particular objects or events. The development of what would become the soliloquy method was influenced by Bernstein's differentiation of *restricted* and *elaborated* codes of language.

Around this time Feuerstein met with members of the targeted communities, consulted with teachers, observed groups of children in instructional settings, conferred with respected colleagues who were also concerned with these issues (see Preface), and began to conceptualize the process of soliloquy in a more systematic and articulated way.

Over the years, Feuerstein and his collaborators continued to develop the processes related to language acquisition, but this volume brings back into bold relief the rationale and practical applications of this approach. One of the consequences of the lengthy interim period was the formulation of the intimate and functional relationship between language stimulation and acquisition and mediated learning experience (MLE), to which we turn next.

THE PARAMETERS OF MEDIATED LEARNING EXPERIENCE (MLE)

Mediated learning experience (MLE) is a vital interactive part of MST. MLE occurs when an intentioned and committed adult poses himself or herself between the child (or other individual) and acts to influence the direct experience of that individual. The relationship is that of the mediator (parent, other engaged adult, perhaps a peer or sibling) and the mediatee (the child, or other object of the mediator's attention and *intention*). The interposition serves to transform the stimuli according to the needs of the learner and the goals of the mediator—to make them more salient for the learner, to direct and focus attention, to broaden the meaning of the experience in time or space. The goals of MLE are to focus attention on relevant and important stimuli in the mediatee's environment, teach skills, reinforce new ways of responding, and the like. MLE creates three transformations:

1. the stimuli are changed in ways that make them more salient for the learner;
2. the learner is changed, acquiring alertness, readiness, and a disposition to receive the changed stimuli, becoming more able to experience new ways of perceiving and responding; and
3. in the mediator, who orients him or herself to the needs of the mediatee following observation, assessment, and engagement.

The development and application of MST rests upon the incorporation of 13 parameters of MLE that have been identified and used by the mediator to orient and organize interventions to bring about changes and/or to enhance the learning experience. They are *parameters* because they do not prescribe specifics—*what to do or say*—but rather guide the mediator to formulate interactions related to the observed and assessed needs of the learner. As you read further in this book you will see how to create an interface between the MLE parameters and the suggestions for ways in which to implement MST, with particular reference to the children and/or situations to which you wish to direct your mediation. To put it another way, the parameters of MLE are not a book of recipes to be applied in a "cookie-cutter" manner, but they are more like the dimensions of a road map that is followed in accordance with preferred routes, conditions of desired experience, and the like. Please keep this in mind as you encounter the many suggestions that we offer in this book!

These parameters of MLE have been richly and variously described in other publications (Feuerstein, Feuerstein, Falik, & Rand, 2002, 2006; Feuerstein, Mintzker, & Feuerstein, 2006), and the reader is encouraged to access them for further elaboration of their applications in different contexts, with additional illustrative examples. A handbook for parents on the application of MLE for younger or at-risk children (Feuerstein, Mintzker, & Feuerstein, 2006) has an extensive discussion of the application of MLE to speech and language development.

In this chapter we will offer brief descriptions of the MLE parameters, and their relationship to MST.

Universal Criteria

These must be present in all mediated interactions, creating the conditions for mediation and oriented toward general development, the comfort and focus of the learner, and creating cognitive structuring of that which is learned. In order for an interaction to be MLE, these criteria have to be acted upon and structured in the encounter.

- *Intentionality and Reciprocity*: The mediator conveys a purpose and direction to the interaction, communicating what will happen, what will be done, and how it will be experienced. The mediator speaks clearly and with explicit detail about what is occurring, where it is occurring, how it is occurring, etc. The verbal interactions of the mediator are directed toward focusing attention and enriching the mediatee's environment. When the mediatee responds, this is reinforced and added to the mediational interaction.
- *Transcendence*: This parameter relates to broader reasons and outcomes, conveying why the interaction is occurring and where it is going, and seeking extensions in time and space ("this is where we have been, this is where we are going, this is why we are going there"). The interaction directs the "here and now" experience toward the future, and looks back to the past. This parameter also encourages the learner to predict what will happen, relates to experiences that have occurred, and enriches the learner's "distance" from direct experience. The mediator encourages generalizations and conceptualizations from the learner's experience.
- *The Mediation of Meaning*: Meaning brings relevance and importance to the MLE encounter. For both mediatee and mediator, this parameter infuses values, validates feelings, and provides the reasons for the interaction. This parameter brings the *"why we do it"* into the encounter. In the context of MST, mediation creates a need—implicitly at first—to participate in the communication, to feel a need for engagement at the receptive level. The role of language is critical here, as these values and attributes are conveyed at various levels of intensity and socio-emotional relevance.

Situational Criteria

The mediator observes and assesses specific situations to determine the mediational opportunities, related to well-planned goals and objectives. If the universal conditions have been established, specific mediational interventions can be related to the situations and events the learner experiences. There is some hierarchy or sequence here, as some criteria may need to be better established before others are presented and engaged. They will be very briefly described, and the reader is encouraged to seek the references referred to earlier to gain insight and details regarding them.

Helping the learner to control behavior through focusing behavior, reducing impulsivity, and monitoring efficient and accurate responding mediates *regulation and control of behavior*. Giving the learner feedback on those skills and achievements that are within the learner's repertoire mediates a *feeling of competence*. Verbal enunciation of what is being experienced creates an inner (implicit) sense of competence—*"I know what is going on, I understand it, I can predict what is going to happen next."*

Involving another individual in an experienced event, eliciting cooperation and empathy, formulating communications that invoke listening, attending, and doing activities that bring individuals together mediates *sharing experience*. As relevance and meaning are experienced, both parties experience being heard, understood, and engaged in a mutually experienced activity. Mediation of *individuation* is conveyed through the valuing of the individual's uniqueness and special qualities—even if they are different from "mainstream" performance or attitudes and values. This parameter is often closely related to the mediation of *competence and sharing behavior*—mediation in these influences and strengthens the others. The mediation of *goal seeking, goal setting, goal achieving, and goal monitoring* project the learner into a representation of the future, and serve to organize and focus actions. The mediation of *challenge, novelty, and complexity* helps the learner to approach, confront, and experience that which is unfamiliar, potentially stressful, or initially outside a sense of competence and comfort (*I cannot possibly do that, go there, etc.*). Mediation within this parameter conveys an optimistic, comforting, and active approach with insight into what has been successfully encountered, how it was experienced, and its implications for further and future experience.

As these situational parameters are mediated, further options to mediate emerge and are integrated into the MLE interaction. They include the mediation of an *awareness of the capacity to change* where the learner observes and accepts the potential for change, and integrates already experienced changes into an altered self-concept:

> *When you said that to me, and expressed your confidence and hopefulness, told me about the changes I had made, I heard it but I did not believe it. I thought about it a lot, and began to think that if you felt that way, and I trusted you, it might be true, and I could accept it.*

Closely related is the mediation of *the search for optimistic alternatives*. This parameter orients the individual to *choose* to be optimistic and positive regarding potential actions or events, looking for and creating optimistic conditions (which were probably available all the time, but not perceived or thought possible). When such options become available, the individual is open to the mediation of *feelings of belonging*, and the learner is brought into the larger community of others—family, neighborhood, culture—to interact and contribute. This parameter is central to the human experience, and to the individual's development of communication (and interpersonal relationship) skills.

MST is made effective because what the mediator verbalizes is guided by the goals and insights that come from MLE. The key to effectiveness is good observation; having a knowledge of the structural and developmental aspects of the learning process being mediated; and then a persistent, adaptive, and innovative approach, all of which we address in the remainder of this book.

MEDIATING EARLY IMITATIVE BEHAVIOR: THE MOVEMENT OF THE TONGUE AS A PRECURSOR OF LANGUAGE

We conclude this chapter with a particularly rich example of the importance of imitation in cognitive development and language acquisition, linking "prelinguistic" experience to the later application of linguistic aspects of MST. Professor Feuerstein, among others (Zazzo, 1962), was always mystified by the phenomenon of intention that was observed in very young children, even in their first few days after birth, exemplified by the protruding of the tongue as an imitative response to the modeling of the adult who is protruding his or her tongue. Piaget considered imitative behavior possible only when the imitator can simultaneously see both the model and the part of the body involved in the imitative act. More recent research (Melzhoff, 2007) has confirmed that newborns are capable of reproducing mouth and facial movements of the adult they are facing.

This is particularly observable when it is done in a way that causes the infant to focus on the behavior of the model (the adult holds the infant's head so as to maintain continuous eye contact). This was considered an important precursor of language development. The mechanism for this behavior is now understood from a neurophysiological perspective (which we will address in the next chapter), and as an important constituent of social cognition and what Gallese (2009) has called *embodied simulation*.

Feuerstein observed that the child exposed to a model of an adult repeatedly protruding the tongue (he systematically observed that it usually required 100 repetitions) begins to prepare his or her mouth, moving and orienting the lips, movements that end up in a protrusion of the tongue. This process has been observed and confirmed by many researchers who have been able to identify this behavior as a "constructive imitative process," differentiating it as *not* occurring in a spontaneous way.

In a sense, one can consider the mother's (or primary caretaker's) face as a *theater* that becomes a source of imitation. Exposure is repeated, there is usually great animation and affection directed toward the child, and thus the conditions for engagement and identification are powerful and "seductive."

The newborn child, in the first few days of life, is certainly not able to "see" his or her tongue, and is thus not able to manipulate the tongue as an imitative response. There have been video-recorded step-by-step micro-sequences of behavior (frame by frame) as the child responds to facial and tongue movements of the stimulating observed adult, by imitating actions that cannot be self-observed.

The same is true of many other processes acquired by the child following exposure to models. These complex behavioral responses (vocal, gestural, gross motor, etc.) have heretofore not been well understood, as the child responds to the model and involves an imitative response, using relevant parts of the body. In our approach, developing MST, we provide a mediated imitation that elicits responsive behavior from the child. An interesting aspect of imitation is how it generalizes to other forms of behavioral imitation, but it is often delayed. This deferred imitation does not occur in response to a direct sensorial experience, but represents the manifestation of internalized models that eventually are expressed imitatively, at other times and in different settings, *in the absence of the model.* In this sense, it can be considered *structured* into the individual's behavioral repertoire, and into the child's neurophysiology. These are our ultimate goals for MST.

CHAPTER 3

Scientific Support

Mirror Neurons and the Neurophysiology of How and Why MST Advances Language Development

HOW AND WHY DOES MST WORK?

There is now very strong scientific support for the theory of MST. If we understand how and why it works as it does, we will be encouraged to do it and sustain it over time and in different settings. For parents, caretakers, teachers, and other professionals, this knowledge should establish a basis for its intelligent, systematic, and persistent use.

At the outset, MST was considered to be a very direct sensorial/ receptive modeling, relying on exposure and repetition. However, there were a number of problems in the attempt to adequately explain how it occurred even though we were confident of responsiveness to mediation. On the basis of clinical and empirical experience we felt the *importance* of the phenomena, and that the process we were describing and applying was needed to enhance the language acquisition of children.

Recent advances in understanding the neurophysiology of brain responses have led to the discovery of what Siegel describes as "neural resonance circuits" (2007, 2010), which include the *mirror neurons* and their contribution to neural plasticity. He summarizes them as affecting, in a reciprocal way (between the parent/mediator/teacher and recipient/ mediatee [our terms]), "imitative, physiologic, and affective enactments" (2010, p. 350). There is much ongoing research extending into many aspects of neural functioning, of which language development is just a part. It is now possible to formulate the importance of MST in the development of linguistic/communicative behavior, receiving confident support from what is now known regarding neural plasticity. Confirmation comes from the results of non-invasive neurological scan technologies such as MRI, fMRI, CAT, PET, TMS, and others that are in states of development, and that were not available at the time our concepts and processes were first formulated. We can now directly observe and understand the neurophysiological foundations of language development, and extend these to cognitive and social development. The relationship between the neurophysiological and the behavioral is now well understood and described (Siegel, 2007, 2010). The senior author, Professor Feuerstein, postulated that there was a relationship between the brain and behavioral experience over 30 years ago (Feuerstein, 1979). Now the available technology confirms his hypothesis.

Researchers can now identify the essential elements of learning experience that contribute to neural plasticity. We will summarize them here, with some reference to their relevance to language stimulation and development. Kleim and Jones (2008) made a comprehensive review of the research, and have identified ten elements that research studies indicate must be present to promote neural plasticity. We will add two more that flow from the first ten, coming from our theoretical perspective and empirical observations. We have developed some descriptive and summarizing labels to serve as a focus for our later discussion of language development in the context of MST.

CRITICAL ELEMENTS IN PROMOTING NEURAL PLASTICITY

- *The Activation Effect*: Research shows that specific brain functions must be activated and stimulated to develop and sustain behavioral functions. We will discuss the physical "activity" dimension later in this chapter.
- *The Specificity Effect:* Interventions need to be specific to the particular cortical function that is the target of behavioral change. There is a relationship between the nature and type of intervention and the resulting plasticity and modifiability of functions. This requires assessment and the provision of activities and patterns of intervention with regard to language development. This has specific implications for how the language of MST is constructed, implemented, evaluated, etc.
- *The Repetition Effect*: Repetition is required for the functional changes to be structurally implanted and manifested in behavior. For neurological changes to occur there must be considerable repetition. However, repetition alone is insufficient, and in some instances can be damaging. There must be variation in task structure to promote plasticity—simply redoing activities without systematic variation is not enough.

- *The Intensity Effect*: Neural plasticity also requires a degree of intensity of repetition. The amount of time spent in practice and contact with the intervention modalities is critical in order to have the modifiability created become established in the neural structures. Cognitive modifiability requires durations of time and intensity of exposure that typically go well beyond traditional and accepted patterns of "therapeutic" application.
- *The Persistence Effect*: Different forms of neural plasticity take place at different times and pacing, requiring *persistence* in treatment planning and implementation over time. When immediate gains are not evident, one must not give up, but push forward knowing that there is a pace of acquisition that occurs, often latently, but eventually materializing. One is often surprised at the gains that emerge after seemingly endless unproductive encounters. When they do emerge, they become a catalyst for rapid and significant changes.
- *The Salience Effect*: The intervention must be important and meaningful. The language produced must be relevant, meaningful, engaging, etc. Interventions that do not convey this element will not be responded to as successfully as those that are meaningful. We describe this as the mediation of *meaningfulness* of exposure. Meaningfulness is directly related to creating awareness, as the learner becomes aware of his or her functioning, of its value, of the changes that are experienced, and of the importance of these changes.
- *The Optimal Timing Potential Effect*: While we do not consider critical periods as a barrier to change, it has been recognized that some kinds of and propensities for change are age related. For example, although it may be easier to induce plasticity in younger brains, the brains of adults and even the elderly are amenable to change. The issue is the level of persistence and effort and the types of intervention required to promote plasticity at various ages and stages of development. The research cautions us not to take the dimension of optimal timing as a reason to withhold or not initiate interventions.
- *The Novelty Effect:* Learning experience must be new and challenging for it to stimulate neural plasticity. If all one does is repeat familiar tasks, learning will be impeded. Challenge and novelty are required, linked to changes and variations in experience. The potential for capitalizing on novelty is endless.
- *The Spread of Effect*: Changes in functions resulting from a particular intervention can affect changes in other functions not directly targeted by the original intervention. This has been described as a *generalization* effect, aided by the mirror neuron systems. As initial MST interventions are offered and are successful, language starts to develop, behaviors start to change, and aspects going beyond the

language behavior alone become evident. Neurologically, it has been shown that activation in one part of the brain will generate activity in other parts, often without awareness or conscious intention.

- *The Selection Effect*: There can be interference, whereby plasticity stimulated or experienced in one area may interfere with changes in other areas. This must be accounted for in the interventions selected, based on an analysis of the needed behavior changes and the tasks selected for the intervention.
- *The Consciousness/Awareness Effect:* The learner must be aware of the effect of changed functions on behavioral outcomes. This awareness serves to reinforce other changes in functioning, leading to engagement and acceptance of frustration and the need for increased effort in response to new stimuli and situations.
- *The Multisensory Stimulation Effect*: Modalities of stimulation should offer many different activations—seeing, hearing, feeling, and doing, leading to structural integration and generalization.

These elements are particularly relevant to the processes of language acquisition and cognitive processing. Siegel points out that "the prefrontal cortex . . . makes complex representations that permit us to create concepts in the present, think of experiences in the past, and plan and make images about the future" (2010, p. 8).

Beyond the normal development of language in children, this has important implications for the use of MST to stimulate and expand language in those for whom language functions are impaired or fragile. Areas have been identified in the brain, such as the superior temporal gyrus (STG) and the superior temporal sulcus (STS), as having an effect on the "mirroring" functions involved in imitation and activation of other areas of the brain. Our knowledge is becoming more and more specific in this regard, and some previously accepted concepts may have to be revised or rejected outright. Our review of the research on the neurophysiology of language acquisition and function later in this chapter bears light on this issue.

MST has sound neurological basis. MST stimulates and reinforces "neural propensities that are set up before birth and then directly shape how we respond to the world—and how others respond to us" (Siegel, 2010, p. 41). One of the direct neural mechanisms for such "shaping" is the action of the mirror neurons, making change possible not only in observable behavior but also in neurological structure and activity—in the language sphere affected by overhearing. There are other mechanisms within the brain as well, relating to the strengthening of synaptic linkages, the simultaneous firing of neurons, and new patterns of neural firing, among others. We will address this more fully below.

THE CONTRIBUTION OF ACTIVITY THEORY TO MST

Activity theory plays a role in language acquisition and is supported by the existence of neural plasticity. As indicated above, physical activity is a central aspect of promoting neural development. Language is deeply related to the experience of human activity. There is an extensive theoretical foundation for these concepts, coming from Piaget (1969), Vygotsky (1956), and the Soviet psychologists embodied in the work of Leont'ev (Davydov, 1988). Language development is closely related to such elements as the development of social consciousness, the acquisition of verbal tools, the experiencing of verbal concepts, and material activity in the context of interactions with other human beings. This is bridged from internal mental activities to elaborated forms of deeper and extended meanings. This leads to an internalization that has implications for both language development and cognitive structuring. It is remarkable how readily young children spontaneously acquire and develop their understanding of the world from the linguistic interactions they observe (overhearing, observing, and engaging). It is also remarkable how closely linked the concepts of activity theory are to findings of the "new neuropsysiology."

MIRROR NEURONS, NEUROPLASTICITY, AND LANGUAGE

While knowledge about these mechanisms is still in a relatively early and not fully differentiated stage, MST relies on the existence and function of the brain's mirroring mechanisms (see Gallese, 2009), whose actions are manifested by the so-called "mirror neurons." However, the process that involves the mirror neurons has been more recently understood to go much further, as part of a more generalized potential for neural plasticity. There is evidence that the mirror neurons are activated by *doing and observing actions that are imitated*. Siegel follows Iacoboni's (2005) differentiation that the mirror neurons are involved in motor actions, while there is a much broader perceptual effect that may not manifest in motor responses. Siegel has summarized these neural functions as "neural resonance circuits" that may include the activation of mirror neurons, but are "activated" even when there is no overt motor manifestation—but other conditions are in effect. The specific neurobiology of these functions is undergoing continual analysis and reframing, and the reader is encouraged to obtain more information on them from researchers such as Daniel Siegel and others who are cited in the references section at the end of this book.

For the mediated effects of soliloquy, the evidence suggests that mirror neurons are triggered in the child's brain upon hearing language, *as if* the child were using these structures him or herself. This elevates the process of *imitative learning* to a very prominent position. Imitation is an extremely important mechanism for the production and presentation of soliloquy, but imitation alone is not enough.

Siegel quotes from the work of Decety and Chaminade (2003), as presented in Siegel (2010), supporting the validity and use of MST:

> Neuroimaging studies strongly support the view that during the observation of actions produced by other individuals, and during the imagination of one's own actions, there is specific recruitment of the neural structures that would normally be involved in the actual generation of the same actions . . . . Such a mechanism would prompt the observer to resonate with the state of another individual, with the observer activating the motor representations that gave rise to the observed stimulus, i.e., a sort of inverse mapping. For example, while watching someone smile, the observer would activate the same facial muscles involved in producing a smile at a sub-threshold level and this would create the corresponding feeling of happiness in the observer . . . Altogether, shared representations at the cortical level . . . would give us a neurophysiologcal basis for the operation of social cognition. (p. 353)

And, we add, in all areas of cognitive development.

The language area in the brain is particularly rich in mirror neurons. The existence of mirror neurons changes some of our long-held conceptions about specific areas of the brain and their functions. For example, it is now known that the Broca's area in the brain is responsible for more than language functions, extending to a variety of motor and sensory reactions—further explaining the neurophysiological correlates to the neuronal mirroring, which we now understand to be central to the MST phenomenon. Moreover, it is now generally accepted that the development of language functions is not limited to or completely localized in the Broca's area of the brain. In fact, the whole concept of localization of functions is undergoing serious challenge (see Doidge, 2007).

The Neurophysiological Basis for Imitation

There is now considerable speculation (see Skoyles, 2008) that the imitative process is importantly linked to motor aspects of speech. When the child is exposed to phonetic input, articulatory processes are initiated. The brain then makes neurological connections that lead to the mimicking of speech sounds (Liberman & Mattingly, 1985). Skoyles offers neurophysiological evidence that imitation in language development goes well beyond—or in our words—*deeply* into the brain. He speculates that "imitation, in spite of playing a mostly transient role in language acquisition, is a necessary process for the existence of speech" (p. 3). Some interesting elaborations of this speculation are offered by Skoyles's review of the research in this area. For example, he cites Miller's (1977) conclusion that "many words that seem spontaneous are in fact delayed imitations overheard days or weeks previously" (Skoyles, 2008, p. 6); and Masur (1995), who pointed out that "at 13 months children who imitate new words (but not ones they already know) show an increase in noun vocabulary at four months and non-noun vocabulary at eight months" (Skoyles, 2008, p. 6). Skoyles summarizes as follows: "speech will arise both evolutionarily and developmentally *around motor imitation circuits in cooperation with those brain areas processing auditory invariants* (and) the processes behind speech will be amodal enabling non-auditory based forms of language" (p. 9; emphasis added). Thus, the child consolidates the imitative activity and uses it both *internally* (thinking and understanding) and *externally* (into linguistic and motor behavior).

Exposure to Verbal Stimuli

These conclusions are further elaborated on and validated by Fogassi and Ferrari (2007), who summarize several important studies describing the effect of exposure to certain verbal stimuli, and to the gestures and meanings that accompany them, as enhancing tongue and muscle activities. On a behavioral level this correlates to activity in the brain, whereby the mirror neurons play a meaningful role in language understanding and neurophysiological activity. They convey the findings of Rizzolatti and Craighero (2004) that when an object is seen, its visual features activate the motor knowledge necessary to interact with it. With regard to tongue protrusion in the newborn infant in response to the modeling activity of the adult mediator, they found an "enhancement of tongue-muscle activity during TMS in subjects listening to words containing syllables that, when produced, require a strong activation of those muscles" (Fogassi & Ferrari, 2007, p. 139). We draw the implication that when meaningful experience is processed by the brain, mirror neurons are activated to support and elaborate the imitative process. Daniel Goleman, in his book *Social Intelligence* (2006), reviewed the research describing mirror neurons as "reflecting back an action we observe in someone else, making us mimic that action or have the impulse to do so" (p. 41).

There are studies that link meaning (in language and speech production) to performance and show enhanced congruence between observation (of behavior) and motor responses (see Bernstein & Tiegerman-Farber, 1997, for a review of language development in both developmental and social contexts, and our elaboration of these aspects of linguistic structure in Chapter 5). This strengthens the linkage—the language, motor, and ultimately neurophysiological mapping—generated by the activities structured in MST. There are extensive research studies that examine this linkage under varying conditions of exposure, and across several primate species, including humans. Considering various aspects of language development, opportunities to utilize both the behavioral and neuropsychological structures to effect change emerge. In areas such as gestural communication (Rizzolatti & Arbib, 1998), the evolution of speech (cf. Mesister et al., 2002; Seyal et al., 1999), and auditory sensitivity (Kohler et al., 2002), the effects of various external stimuli and experiences on neurophysiological processes have been observed.

Another manifestation of the mirroring functions in the brain are the sublingual responses that can be observed by myographic activity of the articulatory system during sublingual speech. This is the phenomenon of muscular activities in the tongue and vocal cavity ("tongue-muscle activity" or TMA) during the child's observation of meaningful activity of others, silent reading, and other similar evocative experiences. Recall our description of tongue thrusting in Chapter 2.

We can now describe how the activity of mirror neurons, as a part of the neural resonance circuits described above, help us to better understand the processes of neural restructuring that we propose occur in MST. Scientists are now convinced (see Rizzolatti & Craighero, 2004) that "each time an individual sees an action done by another individual, neurons that represent that action are activated in the observer's premotor cortex . . . thus, the mirror system transforms visual information into knowledge" (p. 172). We suggest that this occurs in other areas of the brain as well.

In a complicated study designed by Umilta (2001), monkeys who observed activities in which they "understood" the action (e.g., placing food to be eaten behind a screen) experienced a discharge of mirror neurons even though they did not observe the final outcome of the action. When an action was simply mimed—that is, not presented realistically—the mirror neurons were not activated. We can explain this in MLE terms. The placing of the food within the monkeys' view was an intentional act. According to Siegel, "the intentional focus of attention is actually a form of self-directed experience: It simulates new patterns of neural firing to create new synaptic linkages" (2010, p. 41). When the actual action was hidden, a kind of "representational process" was initiated leading to neurological responses corresponding to our definition of "transcendence and meaning." That is, the monkeys "knew" what was occurring, and were "thinking" about the situation, and activating neurological mechanisms as though they were experiencing it—which in fact they were!

Rizzolatti and Craighero (2004), reviewing the research in human subjects on mirror neurons, indicate that TMS studies show "that a mirror neuron system (a motor resonance system) exists in humans and that it possesses important properties not observed in monkeys" (p. 176). Interestingly, humans appear to activate mirror neurons for movements forming (or leading to) an action and do not need to observe the fully manifested action (as do the monkeys). This provides suggestive evidence for the role of mirror neurons in the higher cognitive functions (using properties of transcendence and the imputing of meaning). Other researchers (see Schubotz & Von Cramen, 2001) conclude that the mirror neuron system plays a role in such mental operations as the representation of sequential information that is experienced to varying degrees of direct visual and motor exposure.

An important implication of this work is the linkages that have been demonstrated between action (the doing) and communication (the language), providing what Rizzolatti and Arbib (1998) describe as the link between actor and observer, the sender and receiver of the message. This is central to our conceptualization and usage of mediated soliloquy that will be explained in Chapter 4.

SUMMARIZING THE ROLE OF
MIRROR NEURONS IN LANGUAGE DEVELOPMENT

The research on mirror neurons confirms a reciprocal and supportive relationship between the active (and motor) expression of language and neural development. When language models are provided for the developing learner, neural circuits are activated in the brain that in turn further activate other cortical functions. There is now clear evidence that this mechanism is enhanced by repetitive actions that stimulate imitative learning (Buccino et al., 2004; Iacoboni et al., 1999).

The MLE parameter of intentionality/reciprocity (see Chapter 2) can now be understood in neurophysiological terms. The human's brain "sees" what the actor (the mediator) is doing, and—most importantly—understands and projects why the actor is doing it, processed in the neural system. It can thus be concluded that the conveyed "intention" of the actions plays a very important role in the selective activation of the neurophysiological system. Iacoboni and colleagues (1999) contend that what is mirrored and neurologically processed is not only the meaning of the actions (observed) but also *the understanding of others' intentions* (emphasis added).

This extends to the mediation of empathy and emotional understanding, and is demonstrated by ingenious studies where human subjects were exposed to pleasant and painful stimuli, related to facial expressions of others, and experienced activation of their neural systems in relevant and consistent ways (Wicker et al., 2002; Carr et al., 2002; Singer, 2006). Gallese and colleagues (2004) summarize these experiments by suggesting that feeling emotions is due to the activation of circuits that mediate the corresponding emotional responses. This has far-reaching implications for the contribution of language to social and cognitive development.

Finally, the linkage to language becomes clear. Although there continues to be controversy regarding the genesis of language in the human species, the work of such researchers such as Rizzolatti and Arbib (1998), referenced earlier, provides strong support for the basic relationships of language development occurring as a consequence of the imitation of various forms of language expression. In this respect, the provision of mediated self-talk (MST) receives strong support from the neurophysiological perspective, and its understanding encourages us to use MST systematically and with great optimism.

CHAPTER 4

MST and the Structure of Language

In this chapter we identify and describe structural aspects of language that guide the parent, teacher, caregiver, or therapist, the producer of the soliloquy, to help build a repertoire of verbal skills and adaptive responses. However, our examples are only suggestions, illustrating critical elements of process. The process will be effective and sustained—the adult offering the soliloquy will feel confident, will do it more effectively, and will see increasing and ongoing opportunities—if there is an understanding of the structure and developmental process of language. If I understand that my actions are meaningful and contribute to the child's linguistic (and cognitive) development I will be more enthusiastic, energetic, and systematic in providing it over time and across different situations. If my language reflects critical developmental and structural aspects it will be effective—both in the developmental nature of language experience and in its pragmatic function (it will be meaningful, satisfying, and socially responsive). This awareness is important to overcome natural resistance because of the strangeness of the situation as we have described earlier.

ORIENTING TO THE STRUCTURE OF LANGUAGE

Two perspectives guide MST: (1) identifying relevant developmental hierarchies of skills (or experiences) that should be reflected and incorporated into the soliloquy, and (2) providing specific language experiences reflecting the needs of the recipient, whether to advance language development where there is language poverty or to particularly address such conditions as speech delays, articulatory difficulties, poor syntax, and disabilities caused by conditions of aphasia, dysarthria, and the like.

In situations of special need, one must assess and observe where development has not occurred—through delay or disability, or where the level of performance is limited. For example, many children come from environments where language has been restricted to the minimal necessary interactions, and thus come to school or other social situations inadequately prepared. In such cases the mediator should review expected levels of response and provide additional or more intensive stimulation to overcome limits and provide stronger platforms for further response. Essential here is to direct and modify interventions based on good observation and a willingness to be repetitive, innovative, and engaged in the process.

A number of variables should be considered: the setting or context in which the behavior occurs, the changes in response that are observed, the number of repetitions required, the child's level of attending, physical needs and impairments, and the like. Good mediation requires continuous observation by the mediator—of changes or lack of change in responses, with continual adjustments to reflect what is observed.

This chapter focuses on the language structures that need to be incorporated into MST. Our illustrations are paradigms for what can be done to mediate various structural elements. The provider of MST should use them as indicators or baselines for a wide range of activities that will stimulate and elaborate functions.

PRELINGUISTIC ELEMENTS

For some children, MST should develop a readiness in the child to attend to facial expression (in particular around the mouth). This stimulates the natural process of producing sounds in response to the facial expressions and imitation of sounds emitted by other human communicators. This is an early development—occurring within the first few weeks of life—and occurs naturally in infants as they learn to focus visually (and auditorily) on the world of stimuli around them. As infants are held and fed, as the parental caretaker talks to them and makes a variety of sounds, the process of focusing and imitation is stimulated and reinforced. To make this a process of MST, the parent/mediator undertakes a systematic and repetitive series of actions to intensify the responses and, as the child's awareness develops, converts it into qualities of soliloquy by commenting upon what is occurring, why it is occurring, what is changing, etc.

Here is a detailed example of how this process is constructed and implemented (this example is further described in the case study in Chapter 9):

> The infant is held in such a way that the face is directed toward the mediator, at a distance of about 16 inches, holding the head so that eye contact occurs, and moving the head slightly to restore contact if the infant's gaze shifts away. The mediator exaggerates the shape of his or her mouth, forming and emitting sounds: first, bah, bah,

bah (widening and narrowing the lips, but with open mouth), then boo, boo, boo (with the lips formed into a circular shape), and then bo, bo, bo (with the lips in an exaggerated circular shape and the lips protruding and extended outward). This is done repeatedly, several minutes at a time, over extended time periods, eventually widening and varying the sounds and shaping of the mouth. Within a relatively short time, one observes the infant anticipating the event, starting to shape the mouth—even as he/she is picked up and placed in position, and mimicking the peribucal movements on the adult's face as the sounds are being produced. Focusing of the gaze becomes more consistent over increasingly longer time spans. The senior author [Professor Feuerstein] has conducted clinical research on the role of stimulation such as described above on the number of repetitions needed to elicit the behaviors described. He has observed that children need approximately 90 repetitions with the first sounds, going down to 70 and eventually 30 with continued repetitions and sequencing of exposure.

Relatively soon, this behavior generalizes to the infant attending to other individuals emitting sounds—looking around to find the source, watching the faces of those speaking, and imitating the motor facial movements associated with the sounds heard. Around this time the infant begins to protrude the tongue as an imitative response (see our discussion of this behavior in Chapter 2 and again in Chapter 10). This represents an early recognition of the peribucal movements that are related to speech production.

LINGUISTIC ELEMENTS

An early and important element of soliloquy is the enunciation of an act. Here is an example:

> *I take the glass and drink from it, I bring it to my mouth. I put the glass on the table very carefully, not to let it fall. I am careful to place it away from my arm so I don't knock it over and spill the juice on the table, etc.*

This very simple example illustrates the natural and readily available venues for MST, to be elevated according to the age and situational experience of the recipient. The enunciations of the act are accompanied by the act itself, presented in a way that the child is able to see the act as it is verbally described, follow it, and link together the various demonstrated parts of the action to the words that describe it. The language is clearly articulated, spoken slowly, with exaggerated and embellished qualities (see below), and paced so it will coincide with the performance of the act. The language portrays a succession of acts translated into a verbal/ behavioral modality, according to the particular elements that have to be established or corrected—structured at a level above the child's current presumed level of proficiency, with exaggerated gesticulation and articulation.

The example shows a verbal depiction of an act that is performed, linking the named act to the named performance [including the named object(s) and the other peripheral elements such as spatial relationships, orientation, time, and other objectives]. Linguistically this occurs through the use of adjectives and adverbs, as qualitative elaborations of the nouns (objects) and verbs (actions) that are the syntax of language. The connection transforms the spoken word into an act that is described, giving it meaning and enhancing the ideational process and the meaningfulness of the activity itself.

By enunciating the act the speaker demonstrates the act, names each component of the behavior, and makes the individual hear the various components of the act. But this is only the beginning.

BUILDING THE LANGUAGE STRUCTURE

As we consider the structure of the language to be presented to the child, the following elements should be focused upon and adjusted appropriately:

Appropriate sentence length
Intentionally selected and phased introduction of new words
When to repeat words/phrases/sentences
When to introduce new grammatical structures
Use of idioms and colloquialisms
Vocal rhythm of the enunciation
Pragmatic skills
(all of which will be explained below).

In this way, new language structures are introduced to the child, and linked with cognitive elements of the experience. Related to the structural elements is the need to introduce concepts and linkages bi-directionally— from direct observations of concrete, observable experience (linguistically formulated) and from internalized, subjective experience to direct observations.

This is an efficient way to expose those with speech and language deficiencies to both verbal expression and its motor manifestation—the levels of "doing" *and* "talking about." Here, MST enables us to introduce in a systematic way various linguistic and conceptual elements to be produced by the interaction and to reach out to certain areas of specific needs. The exposure to simple, articulated, repeated language structures is helpful and important. Here are some examples, with various emphases highlighted:

I *put the cup on the table.*
Did I put the cup on the table?
The cup is put on the table by me.
I *did not put the knife on the table.*
I *did not put the glass on the table.*
Should I put the cup on the table or the chair?
I *think it is better to put it on the table.*
The table is bigger and it won't fall over.

Notice the repetition in linguistic form and the direct depiction of the act. When the interaction is in the form of questions, in MST they are rhetorical in intention, presented as thinking aloud (a manifestation of self-talk) and modeling a similar kind of internalized verbalization for the learner. Further, a systematic structure is created that is developmentally organized and oriented to the particular needs of the individual according to needs, limitations, or disabilities.

The soliloquy introduces through self-talk systemic elements of language experience: parts of speech, aspects of elaborated vocabulary, linkages of spoken language to observed and repeated meaningful actions, and the like. It is offered at times when children are naturally engaged in everyday activities. The goal is the creation of an enhanced verbal environment—immersing the child in a verbally stimulating and focused world.

THE NEED TO UNDERSTAND AND
INCORPORATE LANGUAGE STRUCTURE INTO MST

First, why is it necessary to understand the structural nature of language to engage in MST? This question is as relevant for the parent or caretaker as it is for the specialist. Our answer is that if one wishes to stimulate language development in the normally developing child, or assist the learner who manifests delays in language development and acquisition that reflect the normal and sequential progressions of language, and mediate them, one must understand the structural aspects of language. This is necessary to be able to select, organize, produce, repeat, and adapt to changes occasioned by the child's learning and development. This is the essence of the application of mediated learning experience (MLE) to the process of MST.

A Taxonomy of Language Development

To stimulate language development in the normally developing child, or present the learner who manifests delays in language development and acquisition language with models that reflect the normal and sequential progressions of language and mediate them, one must understand the structural aspects of language. In responding to special needs, understanding structural elements becomes even more important. We must understand the structural elements, and then systematically select, organize, produce, repeat, and adapt to changes occasioned by the child's learning and development.

To illustrate and organize this task, we have constructed *A Taxonomy of Language Development*. Our taxonomy is designed to provide the reader with an understanding of the systematic structure of language, as commonly agreed upon by language specialists. Using such a systematic list, MST can be constructed of responses that reflect developmental and systematic elements and organize them efficiently.

In the application of our taxonomy we are less concerned about etiology (causes) of delay or disability, although careful observation and assessment of the sensorimotor, neurological, and biological factors should be undertaken. Different causative factors, once established, will require differing degrees and sequences of mediation, but *do not preclude successful intervention*.

In situations of special needs, where development has not occurred, or where the level of performance is limited (with regard to output or in responses to physical or developmental impairments), the mediator should review expected levels of response and provide additional or more intensive stimulation to overcome limits and provide stronger platforms for further response. As the child's limitations or difficulties are observed in relation to generally expected responses, the mediator adapts the frequency, intensity, and nature of the intervention accordingly. We reiterate: Good mediation requires continuous observation, consideration of the changes or lack of change in response to mediation, and calibration of interactions to more accurately reflect the status of the child and the effectiveness of previous interventions.

Components of the Taxonomy

A first element is developmental stages of language awareness and acquisition. Certain aspects of language must be mastered before efficient acquisition of the next stage. Every language has its own rules of phonetics, syntax, word formation, and speech rhythm. Various aspects of language acquisition require the development of skills, some of which are motor, some are perceptual, and some are conceptual. Speech and language specialists identify five structural aspects that are common to all language types: *phonology, semantics, morphology, syntax,* and *pragmatics.* Our taxonomy incorporates these aspects. We will briefly define each of these terms.

Phonology (the Sounds of Speech). Sound is at the beginning of language learning. Children must learn to distinguish different sounds and to segment the speech stream they are exposed to into units that eventually become meaningful. This leads to differentiating words and sentences. If the infant hears *"thisisacup"* it soon learns to form the distinct units of "this," "is," "a," "cup." Once the child is able to extract the sequence of sounds "cup" from the speech stream, he or she becomes able (with correlative experiences—i.e., drinking from a cup) to assign meaning to the word, and that energizes the next phase, that of semantics.

Infants begin very early to produce sounds. This is called babbling. The babbling of infants is remarkably similar from one language to another. Until the age of about 9 months, all babies "speak" the same way—the babbling of the English baby is very much like that of the Chinese baby. After this age, the sound production of the infant starts to become "language-specific" as the baby is exposed to his or her linguistic environment. This is due in part to the phonemic differences in various languages—for example, some produce sounds that are more "plosive" (front of the mouth, thrusting tongue, lips, and teeth) and others are more "gutteral" (back of the mouth, tongue widened and flattened to produce "softer" sounds).

The development of phonetics in the child's first 18 months is very important. The reason for babbling—the seemingly random production of sounds—is partially genetically coded into a child. Even deaf children start to babble. Babbling in the hearing child occurs because the child attempts to react to and imitate the vocal stimuli of the adults in his or her environment and because the emission of sounds appears to be physiologically developmental. It is not only auditory. In addition to sounds, all children attend to (and start to imitate) facial expressions, formation of mouth and lips, and social interactive contexts. This is why it is important to surround the baby with rich, high-pitched, slow, and highly inflected talk. At first this contributes to phonetic awareness, and then leads to imitation, associational awareness (a particular sound or sequence of sounds leads to meaningful actions—for example, soft cooing sounds from the mother that signal the start of a feeding process), and then reflective speech (a produced pattern of sounds generates that desired action in others—the possibly random production of the sounds "da da" [in the English language context] causes one of the parents [the father] to react in a pleasurable way). At later ages, children will listen and imitate, and then attach meaning to what has been said.

To mediate babbling for the infant and very young child, we start with phonetic stimuli that both stimulate and imitate the sounds that the child emits. For the older, non-speaking, or late-talking child, we use inflection, exaggeration, and repetition to emphasize the phonetic elements of language—for awareness and incorporation into higher levels of language structure. When the infant starts to vocalize through babbling, it is important that they are met with highly positive and active feedback. Infants will often pause in their babble to listen to the mediator, and then respond. Infants respond and learn from high-pitched voices and short words and sentences. Infants will become engaged with the mediator's words, and come to understand what is being said. The mediation is effective if the speaker talks slowly, repeating words, and initially uses simple words with exaggerated inflection—what is often called by adults "baby talk" and language experts as "motherese."

The acquisition of the phonology of the language begins in the womb and is not fully completed until adolescence. Perceptual abilities (hearing clearly, discriminating subtle differences, etc.) usually precede sound production. Anomalies in phonetics, generally based on what the child "hears," can last a long time, and become part of a child's productive vocabulary. One of the authors' children developed the habit of calling wolves "woofs," and walruses "warouses," and his parents tried, unsuccessfully, to correct the pronunciation. People reacted as though it was "cute" and since it was not dysfunctional, it remained in his verbal repertoire well into later years.

Semantics (the Meanings of Words). As the learner is exposed to language, understanding the meanings of words follows, the meanings aggregate into sentences, and the logic and connectedness of verbal communication are learned. Semantics and syntax are closely related in functional value for the acquisition of language—the structure of the language supports the meaning.

The semantic aspect of language involves vocabulary and meaning. In general, the child at early stages makes literal interpretations of words and sentences in context. Linguists point out that a requisite of this understanding is the experience of the "truth" of what is being communicated. That is, what is being verbalized must correspond to that which is perceived, experienced, and affecting the recipient. If the verbalization conveys *"the wind is blowing very hard,"* the learner must experience the wind blowing, see the trees bending, hear the sounds, etc. The further relation between semantics (meaningfulness) and syntax (structure) occurs when complex and novel sentences are understood on the basis of their meanings, and the manner in which they are put together. The basic elements will be the meanings of words, and morphemes (see below). Linguists describe how the learner puts together the constituent elements (sounds of words, meaning of words, functions of words, functionality of the communication) to arrive at "meaningfulness." The meaning of a sentence is a function of the meaning of its parts, as well as the order in which they are placed—this is the general semantic meaning of verbalizations in the system of language.

A first important finding is that the capacity to incorporate new words depends on the capacity to engage in speech repetition (Bloom, Hood, & Lichtbown, 1974; Masur, 1995; Miller, 1977), which leads to "motor vocalization"—that is, expressive language production (Skoyles, 2008). Children learn approximately 10 to 15 new words a day, but researchers have observed that direct instruction (focused mediation) only accounts for a small amount of the new learning (Landauer & Dumais, 1997). These researchers suggest that the great majority of meanings are acquired by what is termed "latent semantic analysis," by which they mean that children experience them in a context and assess what is occurring, then impute meaning in a kind of "rough estimation." This argues for rich exposure, repetition, and modeling of linguistic input, occurring in MST largely through the mechanism of overhearing (as the adult comments repeatedly on the child's experience).

To bring cognitive processes into language acquisition and proficiency, another aspect of the semantic element must be paid attention to. When one understands the "truth" of a verbalization, one can draw inferences from it. This enables the learner to "go beyond" (what in MLE we refer to as *transcendence*) what is directly experienced, and draw meaning to wider and more diverse applications. If the learner interiorizes the meaning of *"the wind is blowing hard"* he or she will make associations to seasons, places where it is very windy, predictions of what will happen to objects caught in the wind, what makes sailboats move, and a wide range of other associations.

Morphology (the Form and Structure of Words). Morphology stands between semantics and syntax—it represents important building blocks toward the functional use of language. This element does not usually come into play until approximately 18 to 24 months of age. The child's working knowledge comes tacitly, meaning not usually through explicit instruction. It is one of the many remarkable phenomena of language acquisition that so much complexity and differentiation occur implicitly for the child, and at early stages of exposure and mental processing.

Morphology is the identification, analysis, and description of the structure of words—the smallest units of syntax. The child learns the rules for how words are formed and used. For example, the child hears "dog" and "dogs" and comes to understand their difference according to a rule (one is singular and the other is plural). They further make a simple analogy when they hear and understand the difference between "dog" and "dog catcher." They learn that words are formed from smaller units, and how these smaller and differentiated units interact in speech. Another term for the smaller units is *lexeme*, which implies the attribution of meaning to the small unit.

There are two kinds of rules that have been identified in the process of analysis. Differentiating "dog" from "dogs" is an example of the *inflectional* rule. This denotes different forms of the same lexeme. When we move from "dog" to "dog catcher" we are using the rule of *compounding*, which forms new lexemes. In general, the process relates to what the child hears, what the child understands (in the context of direct or remembered experience), and what he or she makes of it—focusing on inflectional differences or forming new rules.

There is a third rule that is useful to know—that of *derivation*. It is important because it teaches the child to change word forms through the adding of prefixes or suffixes. For example, the word "independent" is formed from the word "dependent" by adding the prefix "in," which changes its meaning. And the word "dependent" is derived from "depend" and is changed by adding "ent." This is an illustration of the formation of a new lexeme.

The relationship between semantics and syntax is bridged morphology. A caution here—some languages, English notably among them, often violate morphological rules. Thus, one cannot apply them blindly or rigidly. For example, the plural of "dish" is "dishes," not "dishs." Fortunately, in language production and reception, there is a natural blending and flow of expression and experience for both the speaker and the listener, and ultimately the exceptions are learned and integrated comfortably (spontaneously, unconsciously, etc.).

Syntax (*Arrangement of Words and Phrases into Sentences*). There are different theories (and some conflict among them) that explain how children acquire the complex system of visual, spoken, and social symbols that comprise the structure of language. There is general agreement, however, that children appear to acquire the capacity to learn language structures with relatively little guided input. In normal development, researchers agree that children achieve general mastery of the grammar of the "speech community" in which they are immersed by the age of 5 (Crain & Lillo Martin, 1997).

But the nature of the input and the mechanisms for acquiring it are debated—that is, *what* is learned and *how* it is learned. We are interested in the theoretical conceptions only to the degree that they help us formulate linguistic interactions for MST. One theory is "social interactionism," integrating the child's biology (innate capacities) with social interaction. Another theory that has relevance is that of the "relational frame" that is experienced through interacting with the environment. For this theory, the context of language experience is the primary formative factor. We blend these theories together because they seem best to convey a focus on the cognitive processes through which the learner acquires language in response to interacting with the environment—being exposed to the thoughts, feelings, and behaviors that can be conveyed through exposure to linguistic formulations. Chomsky's conceptualization of this process (Crain & Lillo Martin, 1997) suggests a "generative grammar" whereby the acquisition of syntax occurs when the child is exposed to, and selects from, a limited set of choices offered by observing (and imitating) their parents' speech, and relating it to an observed (and meaningful) context.

The various grammatical elements of language—nouns, verbs, adverbs, pronouns, conjunctions, prepositions, and the like—become meaningful, and connect sounds to meaningful objects and events. In a sense, this represents acquiring the "code" of the language, and gradually responding to (and generating) the deeper and subtle means of communication. Thus the structural syntax of a language involves a number of characteristics that can be analyzed by examining the nature of sentences that are constructed—what English teachers call "the parts of speech." Nouns enable us to name objects, denoting specific persons and places. Verbs describe overt actions and inner states of being. A gerund adds "ing" to a verb to change an action (like "to read") into a noun ("reading"). Verbs can have regular and irregular forms, modified by tense (past/present/future), and by rules that seem not to follow any regular logic. A complex code indeed! And when we add the conjunctions, interjections (which are not words at all, but accepted meaningful sounds—"ah," "alas," "oy"), and pronouns it is a remarkable feat for children, at very young ages, to decode and then encode this information.

What is also agreed upon, and what has received empirical support, is that the brain and vocal mechanisms related to it show a gradual adaptation to the use of language, rather than a sudden appearance of skills reflecting the whole spectrum that did not exist previously. The implication from these findings is that language emerges from usage in social contexts, using learning mechanisms that may have some innate constituents (Bates et al., 1998; O'Grady, 2008). There is evidence that children are able, through systematic exposure, to learn the words and syntactical conventions of language, as shown in a study of 8-month-old infants (Saffran, Aslin, & Newport, 1996). Children also acquire "incorrect" structures that they use effectively, showing their capacity to learn structures "on their own."

Pragmatics (Social, Functional Language). Children may have mastered the syntax (long and correctly constructed sentences, consistently correct grammar) but not know or use the social rules for communication. Adults who have experienced brain injury or strokes may also have difficulty with this aspect of language. There are three major skills involved with pragmatic mastery: (1) using language appropriately for different purposes (greeting, informing, demanding, promising, requesting); (2) changing language according to the needs of the situation or the listener (for example, talking differently to a baby versus an adult, giving information to an unfamiliar listener, speaking differently in different settings—a classroom versus on the playground); and (3) following rules for conversation (taking turns, introducing topics, staying on the topic, rephrasing when misunderstood).

There are additional aspects of appropriate social communication that must be mastered. The learner must pay attention and incorporate verbal and non-verbal signals into his or her responses. Social distance—how close to stand next to the person you are communicating with—is an important aspect of effective communication. Tracking facial expressions and eye contact in the listener, as well as content, is also important in framing what is understood and responded to.

The pragmatic aspects of communication vary from one culture to another and from one social situation to another. Efficient communication requires knowing and observing the rules of the partner, and the context in which it occurs. Difficulties in vocabulary or grammar also contribute to deficient or impaired pragmatic skills.

In the taxonomy (Table 4.1) we identify mediational interventions that are linked to the developmental progression of the five functional aspects of language that we have described above. We include age

Table 4.1. A Functional Taxonomy of Language Development

Ages	Phonology	Semantics	Morphology	Syntax	Pragmatics
	Mediation of sounds	*Lexical mediation; understanding the meaning of words*	*Mediation of prepositions, suffixes, conjunctions*	*Mediation of building a sentence: Words in a structured setting*	*Mediation of interactional patterns*
0–1 months	imitate the vocalized sounds of the baby play with tongue protrusion encourage facial imitation make vowel sounds (*ay, oy, uy*) with increasing and decreasing intonation clear view of the mediator's face, eyes, and mouth is a must	introduce meaning to the child's vocalizations		use prosody to alert to syntax—the melody of speech indicates where a sentence ends, where a new one starts apply varied melodies to express agreement, direct attention, alert or soothed, etc.	
1–4 months	mediate repetitive babbling (*pa-pa; ba-ba*) mediate canonical/variegated babbling (*ka-da-tu-ba, te-te-te-ne-ne*) with your face close to the baby so that it sees your peribucal area well imitate what child itself babbles	mediate the child's name many times attribute meaning to the noises of the environment ("Yes, it was an ambulance, *ne-noo, nee-no, nee-no,*" an ambulance)		*It is a doll. A DOLL.* "Baby talk" should come naturally: with a "cooing" pattern of intonation, *high in pitch, with many glissando variations* that are more pronounced than those of normal speech	mediate parent-child, child-parent turn-taking in babbling (*dyadic interaction*) If this "answering back" starts to exist, mediate with intention that by using speech (babbling) he or she can be effective

3–6 months	play with hand put on and taken away from your mouth: (*ba-ba-ba*) in front of the child; play with your lips with your fingers: *"br–br–br"*; encourage babbling, give positive feedback, reinforce when baby does it; encourage baby to listen to own vocalizations, help baby to regulate its own speech organs and muscles	label and show objects and persons to the child (*doll, dad, car*); important to label first and then show the object; create possibly one- or two-syllable words; introduce animal sounds	*It is a doll. Doll.*	introduce *triadic interactions* and joint gaze between baby and parent and the object
6–9 months	continue the above-mentioned	introduce two-syllable words and show objects; mediate *telegraphic speech: "Daddy bye bye, went away."* "Mummy sits. Sits." with the intention of drawing attention to verbs (actions)		play turn-taking games with objects: *"the ball is at me, now it is at you, etc."*
9–12 months	clear and slow articulation should be continued to help to avoid articulation deficits			

Table 4.1. A Functional Taxonomy of Language Development (continued)

Ages	Phonology	Semantics	Morphology	Syntax	Pragmatics
	Mediation of sounds	Lexical mediation; understanding the meaning of words	Mediation of prepositions, suffixes, conjunctions	Mediation of building a sentence: Words in a structured setting	Mediation of interactional patterns
18–24 months	like above	our aim is to go for "naming"—so that the child feels a deep drive to name and label everything in his or her environment	start to mediate posses-sion— My book Kate's bag mine hers emphasize the plural (catS, dogS)		
30 months	like above	A 30-month-old child has about 500 words. Try to go beyond tele-graphic speech (baby sit, daddy do) and introduce and imitate longer words. Try to increase MLU (mean length of utterances) by putting prepositions and conjunctions in front of and between words	Try to increase MLU by putting prepositions and conjunctions in front of and between words (IN the house; the rabbit AND the tiger) Your young child will learn prepositions by hearing them used over and over again, in the correct context; prepositions are said to appear as soon as a child can produce two-word utterances.		encourage to take turns in interactions: appropriate turn-taking behavior and ability to add new info to the ongoing topic encourage to stay on the same topic, to maintain a topic for a longer time

30 months (contd.)	the order of mediating prepositions is the following: space localizers (*on, in, out, at, on top of, in front of, etc.*) *to, from, out of*	mediate the importance of stating the message clearly; create a sensitivity in the child toward the needs of its listeners: even a 2-year-old may repeat or change the form of an utterance if his or her partner does not respond
36 months		
4–6 years	encourage clear pronunciation, learning poems by heart, repeating slogans or songs	
6–7 years	with clear language models give the *"th"* (*thumb*) and *"th"* (*this*)	

ranges with a strong note of caution: They are not included to denote rigid demarcations—that the functions cannot occur before certain chronological periods have been experienced—but rather, these are generally observed periods of time when children show readiness to acquire understandings and requisite functions. More important, the taxonomy is offered to help the producer of the soliloquy to see "the big picture" and place interventions accordingly.

SPHERES OF LANGUAGE DEVELOPMENT

In this section, we address suggested sequential stages of presentation of the language to the child. In the process of constructing the soliloquy, identifying the spheres helps us to plan when to introduce relevant elements and how to organize them into the MST. These are:

Articulation: accompanied by phonemic awareness and production
Enunciation: of objects and acts
Internalization: of that which is articulated and experienced
Attribution of Meaning: developing meaning of what is experienced
     and pragmatic/syntactic usage, with spontaneous elaboration
Formulation of Internal States: accompanied by changes in facial
     expression, proper gestures related to feelings, etc.
Temporal Reference: incorporating past, present, and future into verbal
     interactions
Conceptualization: moving from the concrete to the abstract, from the
     direct to the representational levels of experience

They can be integrated into the soliloquy, facilitating the mediation of structural elements in the development of language (from our taxonomic organization presented above).

The Sphere of Articulation

Here the focus is on the production and reception of the sounds of language. For the child who has difficulty in the areas of articulation, hearing words that are carefully enunciated draws attention to particular sounds that are either fragilely represented or are absent from the child's repertoire. The role of prosody is important here—the melodic cadence of speech (think of the young child learning the alphabet through the singing of the various alphabet songs that exist in many languages). This is especially critical in situations of dysarthria, mild hearing loss, and some early aspects of attention difficulty. This can be used with adults who experience deficits in language production and reception processes following aversive conditions imposed on the brain. For children, many of the songs in the repertoire of parents and kindergartens are very helpful.

Parents should be encouraged to pronounce each word in a way that enables the child to recognize and distinguish (at the level of the phoneme) the distinct sounds in words. One can give (an exaggerated) temporal or intonational emphasis to particularly salient syllables in the communication. Multisyllable words can be enunciated to emphasize—with differentiation over numerous repetitions—a particular syllable, and done so with vocal emphasis (embellishing the syllable of focus, using amplitude, tonality, etc., to focus the child on the sound patterns, positioning of the mouth/tongue/lips, auditory distinctions in sounds such as "p-t," "b-p," and the like). Take the word "telephone" as an example: It can be articulated in various ways, creating phonemic awareness by making conscious and exaggerated articulations, such as:

1. tel-e-PHONE, or
2. TEL-a-phone, or
3. tel-A-phone.

By separating the elements in this way, and repeatedly presenting them, the child begins to hear and ultimately integrate the articulatory elements of the spoken word. The goal here is to create the conditions so the child develops awareness, initiates imitation, and stimulates neurophysiological development through the activation of the mirror neurons.

The Sphere of Enunciation

Enunciating is describing an act or experience as it is performed directly in front of the listener. There are several interrelated levels: paying attention to the action to be performed, the object upon which it is performed, and dimensions of time, spatial orientation, quality, and function. The communication should be structured to increase complexity and abstraction through the inclusion and use of adjectives and adverbs and other parts of syntax, describing the particular act (an example of the mediation of *intentionality*), and can eventually (in the later spheres) go beyond this to the description of ideas, feelings, relationships, doubts, and other aspects of the communication experience (the mediation of *transcendence*).

Here are examples of the enunciation of acts and objects that reflect various elements such as time, space, qualities, and functions:

Time: *Remember the rabbit we saw* **yesterday***? He had very big ears. When you talked to him, his ears stood up straight . . . he* **was listening** *to you! When you see him* **tomorrow***, I wonder if you talk to him* **again***, will his ears stand up again? Let's see* **what will happen.**

Space: **Where** *was he when we saw him? We saw him* **in his cage** *in the garden. I am going to take him* **out of his cage** *and play with him* **on the grass***. We will see how he plays. Look how he hops.* **When he is in his cage he cannot hop. There is not enough room for him to hop.**

Quality: *The rabbit is* **big and fat***! He has* **very white fur. His fur is thick and soft.** *When we touch his fur we can feel how* **soft and thick** *it is. It is softer and thicker than a dog's. It feels more like the fur of a cat!*

Function: *The rabbit has a big nose.* **He uses it to smell everything.** *He tries to smell everything that he sees. He also* **has big ears. That means that he can hear well also.** *His front legs are* **small and short,** *but his back legs are* **very big.** *The rabbit uses his* **big back legs to jump.** *He is a very good jumper.*

Of course, this formulation can be applied to any and all actions and events experienced by the child. Enunciation also includes the *naming of objects*. The mediator shows the object, points to it, touches it, manipulates it to change its orientation, reverses it in space. It is shown, touched, and examined from a variety of directions and perspectives, as a way to make the child focus on both the name and its qualities/attributes, enriching the child's vocabulary.

Focusing on the *action of the object* further introduces its major functions. One starts with objects that have some manifest action potential and have been experienced by the learner. For example:

The cup is to drink water, we use the knife to cut our meat, and the fork to pick up food.

This teacup has a handle because the sides of the cup will be very hot, but the handle will not, so I will not burn my fingers or drop the cup and spill the tea.

Drawing attention to the *function of the object* focuses on categorical and systematic relationships among objects and events that are of a higher conceptual order. The mediator can convey various, more abstract aspects of objects and events. For example: When considering an object (a commonly used implement, an observed object or event) the relationships can be enunciated:

See how this . . . does that . . . I think it does a good job of . . . It is being used in that way . . . Other objects can be used in the same way.

The structural form can be extended: "to drink *from*, to ride *on*, to sit *on*, to cover *with*, etc.," including time, space, quality, and functional characteristics that can be observed, described, and generalized in the experience of the learner. The learner's world is elaborated upon and deepened by this kind of exposure to verbally described activity.

Linguistically, *qualitative descriptions* are expressed through the use of adjectives and adverbs, describing the qualities of the object that include size, form, color, and the quality of the actions undertaken, such as speed, effort, pleasure/pain, etc. This enriches and deepens the child's knowledge of the diverse dimensions of the object, and enables generalizations beyond direct experience—widening the child's sense of the world:

We have seen this before; we will see it tomorrow.

We saw that last week when we went to the park. We rode our bikes down that steep hill and went very fast. When we go to the park next week we will be able to ride the big swing again.

Introducing *personalization* (the mediation of the specific meaning to self and "others") here is useful, drawing attention to and including syntax related to the role of the "protagonist" in meaningful actions:

(You, me, him, your mother, your brother . . .) are wearing a warm, soft, red sweater today because it is very cold outside.

Your mother is very upset because her favorite blue dish, which belonged to grandmother, just got broken.

The producer of MST develops a functional repertoire of nouns, adjectives, and adverbs to present to the child through the modality of the soliloquy, determined by many of the conditions we have described above.

The Sphere of Internalization

The thoughts, feelings, and affective elements of language are distinct from the act of speaking itself but have a meaningful relationship to it. They happen "inside" the individual, at some distance from the observable manifestation of time and space, and yet are related to it as the individual develops *internal language*. The soliloquy should ultimately help the child internalize experience in a linguistic modality. This occurs through the stimulation of memory. How things are remembered, where they occurred, who the child interacted with during the experience, and the like are important qualities.

In language development, syntax and usage are relevant, conveyed through the use of mediational questioning to energize internalized speech:

> *We saw the elephant. What was he doing when you saw him? We were in the . . . the place where elephants and other animals live, and people can see them. In the zoo, some animals have to live in cages, I wonder why? If they are in cages are they safe, and the zoo visitors are safe? I wonder what would happen if there were no cages?*

Open-ended questions and observations do not require an answer, and cannot be answered "yes" or "no." Follow-up questions extend an elaboration of the content of what is being discussed. Notice that the last few examples move the soliloquy into a more interactive relationship . . . the mediator offers verbal descriptions and makes observations that lead to internalization and overt responses when the learner is ready. Even if no verbal response comes, continued discussion—asking and answering questions—has the function of establishing linguistic and environmental awareness and confronts the learner with the need to compare.

Energizing this sphere of language development involves:

Specifying Referents to Action (Nouns and Objects): "Who is doing it? To whom is it being done?" This is often a very difficult aspect of language for children, and it greatly helps focusing and precision to emphasize and repeat relevant referents in the experience.

> *Your father is driving the car.*

> *Your sister has taken your favorite toy.*

Describing the Cause of Action (Verbs): This aspect focuses on the action of the experience.

> *My father is driving the car because he is a grown-up.*

> *Your sister has taken your favorite toy because she likes to play with it.*

Later on, at higher developmental levels, pronouns (*he, she, it, them,* etc.) can add to or replace the referents to increase cognitive distance from the direct and immediately observed objects and events.

Adding Specificity and Detail to What Has Been Experienced: Adjectives and adverbs enhance the meaning of the language, enabling the child to enrich experience, extend focusing, deepen understanding, and think about qualities and aspects of objects and events not previously accessible.

The powerful car runs rapidly . . . the small donkey goes slowly.

The new house is very big.

The fire engine has a big hose on its side to put out fires.

The Sphere of Conceptualization and Formulation of Internal States

As soliloquy moves to higher levels, it focuses on the ideational process and modes of reasoning involving a variety of relationships. Further, it has the potential to include feelings and the reasons or causal determinants of these feelings (moving toward the mediation of *meaning*). This can be conveyed by using expressive mimicry—exaggerated facial expression and noises to simulate crying, joy, confusion, etc.—enabling the child to identify and repeat these aspects through imitative verbal and gestural behavior and through the encouraging (but not by the demanding) of a responsive verbalization. In cases of children with limited verbal ideation and modalities of expression, continued and repeated MST (with verbal and gestural components) is a very rich source of models of behavior.

Introducing Causal Relationships: Moving the language toward the conceptual and cognitive elements requires several intentional aspects:

- Identifying and including observations introducing *teleological relationships*, or the goals of the actions being described:

    I will close the door so that you cannot see what I am doing.

    I am going to fill my glass with juice so I can drink it.

- Explicitly focusing on temporal elements, with concepts of "when," "now," "yesterday," "before," "after," etc., moving toward sequentially ordered behaviors that have time elements as their basis.
- A similar emphasis on adding spatial relationships, or elements of "where" and "how" things are oriented in space. Ultimately these can be combined to encompass three or four of the dimensions— spatial, temporal, and causal relationships. Generally, these

come before the teleological, but contribute significantly to their understanding.
* Enunciating intentions—including feelings and emotions— and describing these conditions relative to the context being experienced. This focuses the learner on the transcendence of language in relationships integrating the past, present, and future into personally experienced events.

Introducing Relational Elements: The language experience can begin to help the learner make relationships among objects and events. A useful strategy is to point out common elements to be applied to a given object or event. For example:

When we set the table for dinner, we need to put out forks, knives, and spoons. The forks should go on the left side of the plate, and there may be a small fork and a large fork. The spoons and knives should go on the right side . . .

In this way, a variety of elements are introduced, and the words/labels/ objects are reinforced by a variety of meanings, uses, and descriptors.

Linking Gesture to Language: Language focuses attention and meaning through the use of gesture. Very early, the child learns to associate motor movement with words and the intention of the communicator. Pointing to the object or person named, or moving one's arms to indicate the speed of an action, intensifies the meaning of what is being enunciated. Elements like time (waving behind the body to signify past tense) or space (using the arms and hands to enclose a virtual space) can be conveyed gesturally. In this way, as the soliloquy is being constructed and conveyed, the systematic and intentional use of gesture enhances the language experience.

In the following chapters we will offer more suggestions and examples of how these structural and functional aspects can be powerfully conveyed using the processes of mediation (MLE).

CHAPTER 5

Introducing
the Child to MST

The application of MST involves two integrated aspects, the structure of the language being formulated and the way it is conveyed by mediating according to the parameters of MLE that we described in Chapter 2.

ASPECTS RELATED TO
MEDIATED LEARNING EXPERIENCE (MLE)

MST is not an incidental or accidental exposure of the child to language. The action of MST is intentional, and contains the three major parameters of any mediated interaction—*intentionality/reciprocity, transcendence,* and *meaning.*

The experience of Umilta's monkeys (2001) illustrates the necessary integration and serves as an example of the linkage between experience and mediated learning. A monkey (while wired to the brain monitors for mirror neuron activities) observes the cracking of a nutshell. This is the *intentional* aspect of the experience—the nutshell is cracked in the animal's vision. It "hears" the cracking of the nutshell. This is the *transcendent* aspect of the experience, as the animal makes a representational association. Last, the animal "smells" the nut being cracked open, which is the *meaningful association* to the experience—it presumably recalls the meaning of the smell. In all three conditions, the animal's mirror neurons are fired.

All three conditions of MLE should be present in MST. In the formulation of the verbal enunciation, the soliloquy (what is enunciated) is done with the intention to be registered (overtly or covertly) and *intended* to affect the individual to whom it is addressed. The mediator formulates the soliloquy according to the goals set for the mediational interaction. What is enunciated is constructed to incorporate its *meaningfulness,* and its relationship to other events or objects experienced in the past or in an anticipated future (mediating *transcendence*).

A NEW PERSPECTIVE ON "INTERACTION"

In the application of MST, the concept of interaction must be thought of in a new way. Because the soliloquy is not predicated on or determined by an expected response from the listener/observer, the effect on the listener is covert—we do not see or hear a response, and the research on mirror neurons suggests the recipient of the input may not even be conscious of being stimulated. However, we know that children attend to stimuli long before they are able to direct attention systematically and engage in overt receptive/expressive communication regarding that which is attended to. With this in mind, the MST is constructed and enunciated in such a way so that the recipient is not required to respond, but is subjected to *conditions* of attending. Thus, the interaction is not contingent on overt indications of whether it has been received, but there is the assumption that it "got through," and that the recipient is affected by it. One can differentiate that which is experienced as "non-responsive or non-communicative" from that which is "non-verbal." The individual may be very responsive, but in subtle and non-verbal ways that are hard to detect.

The groundbreaking work of Rosemary Crossley (1997) on facilitated communication with severely physically and language disabled individuals provides a rich validation for this perspective. The individuals with whom she worked were overtly non-responsive due to their extreme physical disabilities, unable to speak or even bodily respond, but were found to be very attentive and aware of what was occurring around them when Crossley discovered ways of communicating with them. Clearly the mechanism of overhearing language was a critical element in their uncovered but dormant awareness and ability to communicate.

Here is an illustrative example of a child who did not seem like he was paying attention, but was:

> *A student therapist was conducting play therapy, and was encouraged to talk to the child, verbalize observations of the child's activity, comment on relevant aspects of the nature of the activity, and the like. The child was non-verbal, and appeared to be oblivious to the therapist's presence. The therapist complained to her supervisor that the child was not paying attention, and that she was getting very bored from session to session, and thus was reducing the amount of verbal interaction (commenting, observing, expressing her feelings about what the child was doing, etc.). Following this revelation, she appeared for supervision with a big bruise on her head. When asked what occurred she related that she had dozed off in the session, and was awakened by being hit in the head by a wooden block, confronted by a very angry child who yelled at her, "You are not paying*

attention to me, you are not talking to me, I am very mad at you! Pay attention to me!"

These were the first words spoken in many, many sessions, and indicated that the child had in fact been listening to and engaged in the verbal interaction (albeit covertly). This illustrates that the interaction is not contingent, at least at its early stages, on the expectation of acknowledgment—verbal or otherwise. It was quite possible that a great deal of communication had been taking place, but the inexperienced student did not know it. It also emphasizes the importance of enriching and elaborating the interaction regardless of the initial reciprocity of response.

THE STRUCTURAL ELEMENTS OF MST

MST differs from the spontaneous verbal activity that occurs in the context of general interaction. To mediate is to impose actions that have a specific, determined, and explicit focus and goal. The difference is the *intention*. Intentionality is what makes the activity purposeful, and thereby a consciously and systematically structured activity

The mediation of soliloquy, in relation to linguistic and communication goals, specifically has to do with the enrichment of the language of the child by presenting models that have the potential (and goal) of diversifying and elaborating articulation, vocabulary, syntax, pragmatics, and all other aspects of verbal and socially related communication. This is done by applying the structural elements to various immediate and meaningful experiences in the life of the child. We describe this aspect in Chapter 7.

The Direction of Self-Talk

The primary mechanism for engaging in MST in its early stages is that of self-talk on the part of the adult (mediator) and overhearing on the part of the child (mediatee). Self-talk comes from two directions: from the adult mediator toward the child, and the spontaneous and self-directed talk of the child. For the former, what the child "overhears" is eventually incorporated into awareness and the mental structure. Overheard speech plays an important role in language development, as we have described in Chapter 1. The second form is the talking that the child does, to himself or herself, with no evident or immediate intention of connecting with any listeners who may be in the social range, but whose purpose is to consolidate, rehearse, and (if there are others in the range of hearing) be heard by others. At the initial stages the adult's verbalizations are far more important, for they have the potential to draw the child's interest and at-tention, and create awareness and implicit linguistic structures (one ex-ample is how the child gradually learns the referents of pronouns—who are the *hes, shes, thems*, etc.).

The second form is a kind of inner speech that appears somewhat later, reflecting significant experiences of the child that are linked in the child's mind to linguistic formulations. Both forms of self-talk—the adult obser-vations that the child "overhears," and the child's inner reflections that are given voice—are linked to experiences. In either instance, the mediated self-talk process exposes the individual—normally or with expressive and receptive difficulties, or limited experience and exposure—to linguistic formulations for direct experience and models of thinking and communi-cation of verbal behavior. In this way they contribute to what Albert Ban-dura has described as the social modeling of behavior and Gallese (2009) has incorporated into his model of *embedded simulation*—to which he at-tributes "several dimensions of language, the cognitive tool employed to organize, elaborate, narrate and self-consciously structure our own social experiences" (p. 531).

Self-Talk and the Developmental Role of MST

Self-talk is sometimes viewed as a *pre-social* type of behavior, starting at the earliest stages with random sound production evolving into semi-articulated and initially purposeful babbling. As it continues to develop, the child who engages in soliloquy does not address the social environ-ment, but announces his or her observations and ideas *as if* for himself or herself. The child does not talk to a partner (even if one is available in the environment), the talking is to oneself. If the partner interacts or attempts to respond, the young child will generally not consider the response by the partner as triggered by his or her own verbal behavior. Here, the ma-jor function of the child's soliloquy is to consolidate acquired sounds and words by repetition, creating variations of verbal activity and establishing conditions for later (often much later) verbal formulations—at both the receptive and expressive levels.

In situations of immature or inadequate verbal behavior, children interact verbally with one another in very limited ways. The child says something, the other responds in a very different order (often referred to as "poor verbal tracking"), and the dialogue does not at all conform to what we would refer to as a cooperative mode of interaction. One says one thing and the other responds to a different thing. Neither is troubled by this lack of connection. And indeed, soliloquy in very young children is an exercise in verbal expression of fleeting and not very stable ideas that come up in the mind of the child, and the child verbalizes these ideas, externalizes them, or makes himself or herself hear them. Eventually, this externalization of concepts, names, words, etc., becomes reinforced through repetition and some initial observation of the effects on others—eventually added to the conceptual repertoire (the "cognitive structure"). This happens very rapidly and early in the developing infant.

The presence of the child's self-talk (as a developmentally appropriate phenomenon) normally begins to diminish in the child as meaningful, socially interactive verbal communication is established and the child *internalizes* language. If it continues into later childhood or adulthood, it is considered (we think often mistakenly and unfortunately) to be a sign of pathology—think of how individuals who "talk to themselves" are labeled in society. Indeed, those individuals who do not address their speech at the social level are often disconnected from others, and unresponsive to the reciprocity of human interaction. It is important to clearly distinguish the pathological from the developmentally helpful and appropriate with regard to the role and function of self-talk, as the examples we present below will illustrate. In recent times self-talk has been encouraged in pre-school environments, both during pretend play activities (simulations and role playing), and to help children develop planning skills. In this sense, self-talk is a "rehearsal" for future interactive speech.

In order to think one has to formulate one's thought. Self-talk makes the thought audible by expressing it—which is a form of "sharing" with oneself what is noticed, experienced, and then verbally framed and expressed. Developmentally it shows an increasingly precise formulation imposed by grammatical/syntactical structures that are observed and practiced, utilizing the mechanism of imitation. One frequently observed manifestation of the rehearsal and practice at this phase is that children often have imaginary play companions with whom they engage in elaborate and extended verbal interactions. We describe this here and again in Chapter 8.

Here are two illustrations of the developmental function of self-talk in the child:

A young child with Down syndrome would sit for long periods of time and talk to himself. He did it at home and in the classroom. His parents were advised not to be concerned, and not to prevent this self-talk. He was learning language in the best way. When this caused problems in school, and people thought this was dysfunctional, his teachers and others were encouraged to view this as a positive and helpful aspect of the enrichment of his language. It was described to them as a kind of chain of experiences and events that he was thinking about, and putting into a verbal modality. After a period of time he reduced the frequency and the repetition, but it continued as a kind of directed and focused self-talk, and when one listened to it one heard the logical "working-through" of his experience, and the expanding and deepening of his ideational content. Moreover, his peers came to see his verbalizations as helpful to them, and he became a kind of unofficial "class philosopher" as he interpreted to himself, and ultimately for others in his class, the world around him. Today, as a young adult, he has a language that is far more complex and socially aware than is usually found among Down syndrome individuals of his age and older.

When his soliloquy became a distracting factor in the classroom, he spontaneously decided to limit his enunciations to his bedroom and other restricted spaces, where he continued to talk to himself in ways he had previously done more publicly. This showed his growing social awareness in conjunction with his ongoing need to rehearse and master elements of the social situation.

At a given point, he started to direct a virtual group of children, projecting qualities and characteristics of some of his acquaintances. He would organize a variety of events that he planned and directed for this imaginary group, expressed in an elaborate, self-generated soliloquy. He gave orders to his virtual participants and kept a written journal of the "events" that he planned and the orders he gave to his virtual group. Despite the fact that this was largely an imaginary experience, its roots in his social reality oriented his inner process, and had an important teaching and experiential effect on him. He did virtually (as a kind of active rehearsal) that which he could not do in reality, at that point in time—he understood that he would not have been accepted in this role by his peers. But he gained in language, judgment, goal planning, goal setting, and self-image. This led to gradual extension into the real world of his peer environment, as he began to use some of these internally practiced and experienced "skills" in his real-world interactions. Several years later, he is applying many of these previously acquired skills and insights as a youth group leader.

Another boy was brought to us at the age of seven because of a total lack of verbal behavior. As part of the treatment plan offered in the ICELP clinic, he was placed among a group of children who did not speak. He was with them three times a week, for 3 hours a day. They were talked to intensively by the speech and language therapists in the group—every activity and action was verbalized—described, explained, socially linked, and directed. And in other ways they were taught to speak. After approximately 6 months, 80 percent of these children were speaking. This boy was placed in a regular school, and at a given point he started to speak to himself in the classroom, with very peculiar inflections and accompanying sounds. The director of the school called us to say that the boy was disturbed, maybe psychotic, because he "is talking to himself." He laughed at his own jokes, etc. Our response was "Yes, wonderful . . . we have been waiting for this, it is an important development!" We went to the school to explain the significance of this behavior, that "now he is consolidating his speech," that it should be seen as a developmentally appropriate stage for him, and not as a sign of pathology. Fortunately, the school was able to accept it, and the boy slowly reduced the self-talk produced in public, become more verbally directed outwardly toward others, and eventually blended into the classroom group reasonably well.

Another interesting consideration is that of the aged, who often talk to themselves. Where is the pathology? Is it simply a matter of neurological deterioration, in areas relating to cortical control, etc., or is it produced by social isolation, and its effects on the individual who needs to communicate and to manifest links to the outer world, and talks to himself or herself as the most available subject to which the communication can be directed? There may well be some neurological factors involved, but they do not preclude using the positive benefits of the MST approach to stimulate and perhaps even restructure the neural system.

PUTTING MST INTO PRACTICE

The application of MST relies on using MLE as an essential vehicle for the interaction. As such it must be:

Planned: having an objective (goal) that we want to occur in a specific age/level/sequence;

Systematic: applied in a thoughtful, organized, and articulated manner, in relation to goals;

Consistent: repeating the same techniques, in the same ways, for the same behaviors and settings;

Flexible and Adaptive: making adjustments in response to changed conditions or responses; and

Directional: focusing on goals, and orienting responses in light of them, clearly articulated to the learners and "significant others" in the environment.

The general objective is to expand the child's verbal exposure by varying content and level of complexity. The adults in the child's life (parents, siblings, and others) can develop soliloquies that reflect the qualities described above. When soliloquy is put to the service of improving any of the child's language deficiencies (articulation, sentences, syntax, etc.) it must reflect the appropriate structural elements to mobilize the child's cognitive and interactional skills. The "starting point" is the enunciation of actions that are then used with the child to rehearse, calibrate, and repeat that which has been experienced and expressed (see Chapter 4). This chapter and Chapter 7 identify relevant structural elements and show how they can be conveyed effectively.

Ultimately, for MST to be useful for the child, there must be an attraction to listen to what is being said, and therefore the exposure must be interesting, meaningful, and convey energy and engagement. This occurs through the mediator's *intentionality* of focus upon skills or concepts that are relevant. When this is successful, interest is enhanced and the mediator can slowly increase the complexity of the language structures, using targeted words and concepts, with appropriate repetition and elaboration. This leads to a deepening of the communication/verbal experience that the child cannot have access to otherwise—conveying feelings, meanings, projections, expressions of happiness/sorrow/confusion, etc. The whole gamut of affective experience relies on an initial level of interaction, which serves as a platform of readiness for this necessary further development.

NORMAL VERBAL INTERACTIONS VERSUS REMEDIAL OR THERAPEUTIC APPLICATIONS

MST can be applied in normal social and behavioral situations, or in more structured therapeutic interventions. The therapeutic application of MST is directed toward individuals with special needs to develop language in response to delays, dysfunction, or deterioration. However, we feel an important distinction must be made. While the approach clearly has relevant applications in therapeutic interactions (e.g., speech and language therapy), it should not be restricted to the therapeutic setting. MST is designed to be provided in the normal and natural experience of the child. This does not mean that it cannot or should not be used in the therapeutic context as well, and in conjunction with normal day-to-day experiences of the child (as several cases in Chapter 10 illustrate).

Why do we raise this caution? If the exposure is *restricted* to the therapy modality, the interaction will be limited to the therapist and client, and directed toward and limited to a specified range of tasks/activities, and confined to the usual 1 to 2 hours per week. Given the many natural and available opportunities for its introduction into the child's life, MST can amplify the exposure to a very large variety of experiences otherwise inaccessible, every day, and in a diverse range of available settings.

In situations both of normal and regular interaction and the more focused therapeutic environment, the individual is given an opportunity simply to register by listening and observing what is being expressed regarding behavior or events. In addition to the regular day-by-day interaction potential, another useful strategy is to place children with speech difficulties with children speaking normally. They are thus exposed to a rich environment of "non-demand" models of verbal and social interaction with peers, and will use the overhearing and imitative potential of the experience to add to their internalization of language.

DIRECTING MEDIATION TO LINGUISTIC ELEMENTS

We are now in a position to elaborate on our working definition of MST: the accompanying of words with the execution of certain acts that are experienced and potentially meaningful for the child, intentioned by the selection of stimuli, and conveyed in a way that creates both extended meaning and further understanding and action.

For this definition to be meaningful, we review the essential elements of the linguistic experience incorporated into MST: there must be *enunciation* of the action, presented in a *rhythm of speech* that attracts attention and motivation, actions and related language should *substitute* for the child's direct experience, there must be *repetition with variation and conceptual elaboration*, and elements of *time, space, causality, and emotional attribution* must be included.

DEVELOPING SOCIAL AND EMPATHIC AWARENESS

Interpersonal awareness and social skills are aspects of cognitive development. Neuroscientists are beginning to recognize and find structures in the brain to explain these functions. They acknowledge the formative role that language development plays (Gallese, 2009). MST contributes to this development in major ways. Language development is intimately linked to social development—learning to understand the other, their goals and reasons for their actions, and the relationship of the actions of others to the needs and behaviors of the self. The role of MST is to make the verbal interaction—first through modeling and ultimately through imitation and elaboration—intentional, directional, and meaningful. An *orientation and need* for reciprocity are stimulated by the exposure. The child is made aware of how and why someone in his or her direct experience is acting in the way that he or she is. Even more so, with this comes an awareness of the stimuli impinging on the individual. Mediation transforms these stimuli by creating specific characteristics and stimulating awareness and consciousness of the reasons why the mediator is being explicit and focused, and conveys an explicit intentionality in word and action:

> *I am feeling very sad. I have lost my dog . . . he has not come home.*
> *I wonder whether he has been hit by a car.*
> *I wonder if he is cold, hungry, frightened about being lost.*
> *Should we go out to try to find him? Where should we look? Should we*
>   *wait until morning to look for him? Will it be too late . . . ?*

The critical concept is that of awareness and consciousness (see one of the cases in Chapter 10). There is increasing evidence that empathic awareness is activated in areas in the brain leading to higher-level cortical functions. We have already referenced the work of Gallese, Siegel, and Goleman, who have summarized and extended our knowledge of these functions. This extends the potential frontiers of MST, as we will consider in the chapters that follow.

CHAPTER 6

Putting Soliloquy Into Practice

For Parents, Teachers, and Care Providers

You are a parent, sibling, care provider, teacher, or professional who wants to do soliloquy, or mediated self-talk (MST) as we have described it in this book. You want to generate a language environment, on a daily basis or in a wide range of general and informal interactions. The questions are *what to say, when to say it, where to say it,* and *how to say it.* This chapter offers a number of suggestions and model responses, focusing on the practical language and social interactions that children and others engage in as they experience daily life in families, school, the community, and other venues.

OVERHEARING IS THE PIPELINE OF SOLILOQUY

Our suggestions focus on the practical language and social interactions that children and others engage in, as they experience daily life in families, school, the community, and other venues. We remind the reader of the "non-responsive" expectations of the soliloquy. We reiterate this expectation by emphasizing that the power of MST is precisely in its generation of verbalization (language structures and content) especially when the child is not overtly focused—inattentive but within the sphere of reception. The point of MST is to provide parents, teachers, and others the reason and responses to talk to themselves (the "soliloquy"), not related to whether the child will or will not respond, or even seem to pay attention. This self-talk will effect a neurological learning process for the child, and the activity of providing the language in a meaningful context is an important aspect of the eventual neural structuring.

Understanding some of the linguistic structures that have been identified can guide our interventions according to the readiness and developmental needs of the child—but we should not be a slave to them. It is important to know the child or children, and use our intuitive sense of what is appropriate, given our observations of the context of interaction and the nature of the child or children we are interacting with. When we intervene, we often find ourselves surprised by results that contradict some of the experts' conventional wisdom.

We return again to the role of *overheard language* in the production of MST. Overhearing is the pipeline of soliloquy, but it is not in itself mediating. There needs to be intentionality and particular goals that underlie the provision of MST.

WHERE TO DO IT?

There are two places where soliloquy can be offered: (1) the natural occurrences of daily life, and (2) in specially planned and organized experiences.

The most natural venue for interaction is around the shared daily routines of family, school, and community life. They abound with opportunities to generate language that is descriptive, explicative, and directional.

If the mediator wants to expose the child to particular aspects of language experience, providing new or engaging content, intensity, complexity, etc., specially planned or unusual experiences offer an opportunity to experience and link language to awareness and competence. The example that follows shows the relationship of language to cognition that is the rationale for the use of MST.

We recall being with a child as we watched a small airplane land on a lake, using its pontoons to float toward the shore. We described the plane's landing, contrasted landing on the ground versus landing on water, how the plane floated, why it would do as it was, and so on—with the child generally listening but not responding, and being distracted by all of the other stimuli around him. As the adult was talking, the airplane came toward the shore, and then up onto the shore, using the wheels that were attached to the bottom of the pontoons but could not be seen. The child was startled, fearful (the loud noise and unexpected movement), and then focused. The child did not verbalize, and attention wandered as the events occurred. Later we were surprised at the questions the child asked for several days afterward, especially since he did so little verbalizing during the direct experience.

Imagine the power of this event as a specially planned experience, designed to give the child a particular exposure under conditions that provide opportunities to reinforce or elicit learning—assimilating what is seen and heard, accommodating to new and different experiences. Trips to the zoo or museums, visits to extended families, vacations to new or unusual places—all of these can be put into the framework of a specially planned experience, if the mediator identifies and acts on the potential of the venue, and is oriented to the needs of the child.

PREPARING FOR MST

We first must think about the range of natural interactions and shared experiences that provide opportunities for soliloquy. Every aspect of daily life can be a focus for preparing self-talk—waking up in the morning, going to sleep at night, brushing teeth, putting clothing on, every aspect of mealtimes, trips to the market or the playground, and many more. Similarly, teachers can use experiences like lining up for gym; observing fish in a classroom aquarium; preparing for, experiencing, and reflecting on a field trip; developing classroom projects; preparing for holidays; organizing materials for learning; or preparing to go home for the day. Because they are so "natural" we often do not think about these experiences in the context of MST, but at the same time may apply aspects of MST to them spontaneously.

Because of its very "naturalness," the need for this must be understood and practiced—to justify doing the self-talk, which at first may feel artificial and unnatural—so that it becomes a natural and almost automatic response and without focused awareness. As we indicate elsewhere in this book, it is important to be intentional, systematic, persistent, and repetitive. The essential element is that the provider thinks about the structures of language, the situational opportunities, and the needs and objectives of the child or children to whom the mediation is directed. Doing so creates a sense of purpose and comfort, so that the verbalization becomes natural, automatic, and repeated, applied in a variety of situations. An effective use of MST occurs when parents, teachers, and caregivers are able to bring new elements to innovate and elaborate on the child's cognitive awareness of language.

AN EXAMPLE OF MST IN A FAMILIAR, DAILY-LIFE ENCOUNTER

A good way of understanding the process and preparing for it is to take one natural occurrence and analyze it in several ways: (1) what are the tasks or skills required in it, (2) what are the events that occasion it, (3) what is the mediator's natural role in the interaction, (4) what is the temporal and spatial nature of the context in which it occurs, and (5) ultimately, how can it be labeled and described in a way that is consistent with the child's linguistic development (on a receptive level)?

Our example is familiar for every family—waking your child up in the morning and getting ready for the day (in Chapter 9 we provide a parent's description of another familiar everyday opportunity to engage in MST).

1. *Tasks/Skills:* "It is morning. The sun has come up. We will need to get out of bed and get ready for the day. Today is a school day. We must select the clothing we will wear, wash ourselves, and brush our teeth. We must do it rapidly so we do not miss the bus that will take us to school . . ."

2. *Events That Occasion the Activity:* "Today is one of our school days. It is your friend's birthday. We have a present to give. There will be cupcakes to eat. We will bring them for the class. Perhaps there will be balloons and special music. I remember when it was your birthday . . ."

3. *Mediator's Role:* "I will help you wake up. I will open the curtains and turn on a light. We will go to the bathroom together so I can give you the toothpaste and brush. I wonder whether you will need help putting the toothpaste on the brush . . ."

4. *Temporal/Spatial Elements:* "First we will need to make sure our eyes are open and no more sleepy face. Then find our slippers so that the floor doesn't make our feet cold. The bathroom is down the hall . . . we should get there before your brother does or we will have to wait . . ."

5. *Labels and Descriptions:* "You have red slippers and brown ones with bear faces on them. Which shall you choose? You have a new red toothbrush and you can use it or your older green one. The toothpaste tube is almost empty . . . I wonder whether there will be enough left this morning, or we will have to open a new tube . . ."

These kinds of verbal interactions can be done at early ages, long before the child can be assumed to have internalized receptive language structures, and without regard to whether the child appears to be listening or is able to respond. Some of the critical aspects of this example are verbalizing in a low-key, non-demanding way, in a gentle rhythm, as a self-reflection that the child hears. Our self-talk presents the parameters of an experience that the child will assimilate. If the child overhears and observes what is being said and done the brain is stimulated and activated to store and imitate that which is observed.

MST IN SPECIALLY
PLANNED EXPERIENCES

In addition to natural occurrences, we can create some specially designed experiences that offer opportunities to verbalize aspects of observations or activities that are not available in the more natural and familiar venues. A trip to a zoo or museum offers opportunities to label objects, describe their qualities, compare attributes (*the giraffe is tall and thin and the hippo is short and fat*), identify feelings (*that lion is scary, the monkey is funny and makes us laugh*), and so on. When one goes beyond soliloquy into responsive interactions, such special events can be considered and structured for what the parent wants to have happen in relation to well thought out needs of the child. In a newly published book, *What Learning Looks Like*, Feuerstein and Lewin-Benham (2012) describe the many opportunities and strategies to take advantage of such events. Following such experiences, we can encourage children to recall objects and events, and can find books or videos that recreate or expand upon the experience.

ADAPTING AND INNOVATING

Throughout the doing of MST, we must be inventive, adaptive, and responsive to our observations of needs and responses. The many suggestions that follow are not meant to be taken as a "cookbook" of recipes that must be followed. Rather, they are illustrations and examples to be designed for and adapted to the specific, "real-time" activities that are being experienced by both adult and child. MST works best in a climate of creativity and innovation—seeing things in new, unusual, or humorous contexts, and in bringing as much enthusiasm, inflection, and exaggeration into the verbalization as possible.

In this latter regard, MST is enhanced when the mediator is relaxed, playful, and intense, elaborating pronunciations, making oneself almost sing the words, and varying the rhythm and inflection of the vocalization. This adds to the variations, and focuses attention on aspects of words and concepts. This may feel awkward and unnatural, and may be contrary to one's normal verbal and reactive style. We may have to "transcend ourselves," going beyond our natural response tendencies as we do when talking to an infant, or a puppy! We believe that these are skills to be learned and practiced.

THE VERBAL ELEMENTS OF SOLILOQUY

In this and the following sections, we offer many suggestions and illustrations. They should be viewed as a scaffold or a skeleton, upon which the "decorations" and "meat" must be added. We consider that these elements are in a general order with some hierarchy—things to be done before other things.

Our intention here is also to translate linguistic elements into very practical and functionally available examples.

Naming Objects

Objects in the child's view should be presented and named, with appropriate gestures (pointing, touching, holding, etc.). In the beginning they should be simply named. Later they can be described according to their characteristics—big or small, their colors, what they feel like to the touch (soft, hard, rough, etc.), whether they have been seen before and where they were seen, etc. The objective here is to increase the number of sources of information to attend to.

We start with salient objects—the light from the center of the room, the chairs, tables, implements on the dining table (plates, dishes, cups and glasses, eating implements such as knives, forks, spoons, etc.), and the like. The naming should be accompanied by inflection and emphasis that draws attention to the structure of words, their phonetic elements, and so on.

*This is a **taaa**-bull (table).*

*This is a sp-**ooon** (spoon).*

*Look at the **light**. Where is the **light**?*

By naming the object, it can be shown, touched, and examined from a variety of directions and perspectives, as a way to make the child focus on both the name and its qualities/attributes.

*Now I see the **rabbit**.*

*The rabbit is **big and fat**.*

*Now I see his **fur**.*

*You can **touch his fur, feel how soft it is**. Is it like a cat's fur, or a dog's?*

*The rabbit has a **big nose** to smell well.*

*He has **big ears** to hear sounds well.*

*But his **back legs** are so big, so he can jump well.*

*He has **sharp teeth** to eat the carrots he likes.*

Introduction of Verbs

These examples introduce the qualities and functions of the object, leading to establishing (later) higher-order concepts. The structural form may be extended with other words that extend the meaning: "to drink *from*, to ride *on*, to sit *on*, to cover *with*, etc.," conveying aspects of time, space, quality, and functional characteristics that can be observed, described, explained, and generalized to other similar objects and events in the experience of the learner.

*The powerful car **runs rapidly** . . . the small donkey **goes slowly** . . . the new house is very big. . . the fire engine has a **big hose** on its side to **put out fires**.*

This is the "doing" that occurs in relation to objects and events in the experience of the child. This element emphasizes action word(s), and should accompany them with relevant and appropriate gestures (exaggerated and embellished as much as necessary and appropriate). At this level, the goal is to link action to objects.

Verbs also focus on the cause of action. This is another important aspect of linguistic and experiential precision. This aspect of language expression focuses on the action of the experience.

*My father **is driving** the car.*

*Your sister **has taken** your favorite toy.*

The action word or words should be embellished, emphasized through an amplified voice, facial expressions, and changes in rhythm.

*I **lift** the spoon . . .*

*I **turn** the light on . . .*

*I **push** the baby's stroller . . .*

The syntax can be made more complicated with grammatical constructions of more complexity, such as:

*I lift the spoon and place it on the table, next to the knife, and put it on the
left side of the plate.*

The action of the object introduces its major functions. One starts with
objects that have action potential in some way, and have been experienced
by the learner. For example, a familiar object's functions can be enunciated:

*The cup is to drink water from, the knife is to cut our meat with, the fork
is to pick up food with. I am putting this hot tea in a cup with a handle, so
I can pick it up without burning my hands. If I put the hot tea in a glass I
cannot lift it because it will be too hot.*

As a further example, the naming phase can be elaborated on to include action and function:

*I pick up the fork . . . I am using this fork to pick up my food . . . I use the
fork and not my hands . . . with the fork I will put the food in my mouth,
and then use the fork again to pick up more food when I am ready to eat . . .
I can do it many times, again and again, etc.*

Adding Qualities to Objects and Action (Adjectives and Adverbs)

These elements embellish meaning. They draw attention to qualities
of the enunciated objects and actions—their size, color, weight, intensity,
etc.—and help the child to differentiate them in awareness. The world
becomes more detailed and more ordered by the qualitative descriptions
that are added to the child's verbal repertoire.

Initially, the attributes should be clearly observable to the child—
concrete aspects that can be directly experienced. Later, more subjective elements can be included. For example, if something is described
as "heavy" its qualities should be made clear and even exaggerated in
movements to indicate the effort required to lift its weight:

*The **big** spoon is **heavy**; the **small** spoon is **light**.*

*I must reach **up very high** to turn the light on.*

*The light that I turn on is **very bright**.*

*When the baby is in the stroller, I must **push very hard** to make it move.*

Qualitative descriptions are expressed through the use of adjectives
and adverbs, describing the qualities of the object that include size, form,
color, and the quality of the actions undertaken, such as speed, effort,

pleasure/pain, etc. This enriches the child's knowledge of the diverse dimensions of the object, deepens their understanding of it, and creates conditions to generalize beyond the direct experience: verbal utterances that widen the child's sense of the world take the form of such structures that move content into an expanded sense of time and space:

> *Where have we seen this before, when have we done something like this, will we encounter it in the future, etc.? We saw that last week when we went to the park. We rode our bikes down that steep hill and went very fast. When we go the park next week we will be able to ride the big swing again, etc.*

Referents and Personalization

Introducing the specific meaning of objects and events to ourselves and others draws the child's attention to, and includes syntax related to, the role of the protagonist in meaningful actions.

> *I am wearing my warm, soft, red sweater today because it is very cold outside.*

> *You are wearing a heavy coat because you are colder than I am today!*

A related aspect of this level of language structure is the specifying of referents to action (nouns and objects). In addition to adverbs and adjectives, focus can be added on the referent:

> *Who is doing it? To whom is it being done?*

This is often a very difficult aspect of language for children, and it greatly helps focusing and precision to emphasize and repeat relevant referents in the experience.

> *Your **father** is driving the family car very fast.*

> *Your sister has taken your **favorite toy** and now you cannot play with it.*

Adding Specificity and Detail to That Which Has Been Experienced

In addition to the adjectives and adverbs that enhance the meaning of the language, the soliloquy can enable the child to enrich experience (extend focusing, deepen understanding, think about qualities and aspects of objects and events not previously accessible) and thereby consider aspects that elaborate on the meaning of what is directly experienced. There are many opportunities to integrate the descriptive elements with other dimensions that are relevant to the linguistic formulation—comparisons of qualities (*big and heavy, small and light*), degrees of the attributes (*very bright*), amount of effort related to the weight of an object. Others are possible, but we include these to show the ways in which the linguistic formulations can be made more complex, leading to increased cognitive functioning.

It is important to emphasize here and throughout this discussion the necessary and intimate relationship of language exposure and experience to concept development.

Enunciation of Acts

This element brings together the previous dimensions, linking the object and the action into a causal and meaningful sequence. For example, if "table" and "spoon" have been used, then the phase *I put the spoon on the table* will reinforce and explain the action, and connect the object to the action—at first because it is happening in front of the child, and later as an abstract recollection, distant in time and space.

Describing the action introduces the element of causation. Later on, at higher developmental levels, pronouns (*he, she, it, them,* etc.) can replace the referents to further increase cognitive distance from the direct and immediate experience of objects and events.

Enunciation of actions presents models that have a coherence and meaning for the observing child.

Now I will turn the light on. It is getting dark and hard to see well.

I am picking up the glass and drinking from it. I was thirsty. I want more.

I am lying on the bed. My pillow feels soft and smells good.

Gestures add to the enunciation of actions, strengthening the meaning and relationship of the actions. They amplify the actions. We know that the brain mimics (through the mirror neurons) actions that are observed, especially when they are meaningful. So when the phrase *I turn the light on* is accompanied by a gesture of turning the switch, the child makes a sustained connection between the words and the action and a neurological process is initiated or reinforced.

Temporal and Spatial Elements

Placing objects and events in time and space helps the child to differentiate immediate (direct) experience, and move to more distant encounters. This creates cognitive distance. If the child is exposed to linguistic formulations that reference that which occurred in the past, and that which will happen in the future, their ability to transcend immediate experience is expanded, and they "represent" in their minds what is being experienced. Thus, temporal aspects of experience are both an integral aspect of language development and a crucial element in extending cognitive functioning. Think of a spotlight that shines on what we immediately experience and can be focused behind us to "see" what we experienced previously, and ahead to get a glimpse of what is coming.

These elements are naturally part of verbal formulations.

*We did that **last week**.* [past]

***Now** we are going to do something.* [present]

***Later** we will do something else.* [future]

Descriptions of the actions of others placed in a temporal orientation helps to predict future actions or explain what previously occurred:

***Today** is your first day at your new school. You will have to find your new classroom and meet your new teacher.*

*Sally went to school **yesterday** even though she had a headache.*

*Your brother must do his homework **this afternoon** because he has basketball practice this evening.*

*We saw a film on television that showed an asteroid coming to hit the Earth. Do you think that something like that **could happen**?*

Even words that do not have an explicit temporal quality convey aspects of time, like the phrases "this afternoon" and "this evening" in the example above. Think of the words "twilight" and "sunrise."

Another element is that of where things are oriented in space. Concepts such as *above/below, in front of/in back of, inside/outside/next to/in between,* serve to orient the learner to awareness of where one is in the environment. Spatial elements can be integrated into other verbal formulations, or can be isolated for emphasis or repetition:

*I place the doll **on** the chair.*

*I put the ball **under** the table.*

*The toy box is **under** the bed. I am taking it **out** and putting it **on** the bed.*

*I am taking the dog to the **back** door of the house to go **outside**.*

At later stages, time and space can be combined. This combination is good for cognitive development, increasing the child's ability to pay attention to multiple sources of information, and widening the mental field. Here is a soliloquy developed for a child playing with a dollhouse (putting many of the dimensions together):

> Let's play with the dollhouse. I **am opening** the **back** of the house so we can see all the rooms. I **am going** to **put** the child dolls in the playroom, and the father **in front** of the house because he is **coming** home. The mother **is cooking** in the kitchen, but **soon** the table for dinner must be set. Who **will do it**, and **when will it be done?**

Gesture, Mimicry, and Non-Verbal Communication

Language is greatly enhanced by the use of gesture. Very early, the child learns to associate motor movement with words and the intention of the communicator. Pointing to an object or person named, or moving one's arms to indicate the speed of an action, intensifies the meaning of what is being enunciated. Even elements like time (waving behind the body to signify past tense), or space (using the arms and hands to enclose a virtual space) can be conveyed gesturally. As the soliloquy is being constructed and conveyed, the systematic and intentional use of gesture should enhance the language experience.

COGNITIVE ASPECTS OF VERBAL FORMULATION

In this section we will briefly describe some additional aspects that add to the cognitive development that is related to language exposure and acquisition. Remember that MST is also directed to older learners and adults to address their language needs.

Quantities

The question of "how many?" can be associated with objects and experiences. This relates to counting, grouping, and ultimately to summative behavior. Adding the quantitative dimension of a description meets this goal:

> I am picking up **one** fork at a time until I have the **four** that we need for those who will eat dinner with us.

Summative behavior is a higher-order cognition:

There are five people in line, and only four ponies. Do you think that we will have to wait for the next turn?

Cause-and-Effect Relationships

Very early, children can understand simple causal relationships, and begin to differentiate direct causation from coincidence. This can be integrated into verbal formulations:

*I am holding the glass very carefully because if I drop it and it hits the floor **it will** break, and we **will have** to get the broom and sweep it up. And besides, Mother **will be** very upset because it is one of her very special glasses.*

We have emphasized causal language in this example because we want to illustrate the mental operations of formulating hypotheses (*if/then* thinking), considering their reasons, estimating outcomes, and the like.

Comparative Observations

Comparison is a basic mental operation, and much other thinking depends upon it. Comparative thinking is not automatically present in children's cognition. Some children observe without comparing. In early verbal formulations, simple comparisons of size, shape, color, or number can help the child differentiate his or her world.

These aspects enrich the descriptive qualities we attach to language, stimulate a deeper awareness of the objects and events in the child's world, and serve as a platform for other and extended cognitive functions.

Understanding Intentions

This is the predictive and subjective quality of directly observed actions. What is the action that is taking place, why it is occurring, and what might be some of the expected outcomes? It is interesting that the simplest actions do not automatically lead the child to this inductive level of thinking. Our linguistic formulations can bring children to this point:

I am putting the clothing in the washing machine. I must make sure that the clothing is not all on one side or the machine will not run smoothly. I must put the soap in after the clothing, and spread it around the top of them, or the soap will not clean all the clothing . . .

This must be done intentionally, explicitly, repetitively, and for very routine experiences in the life of the child.

Building and Connecting Sentences

At the beginning, sentences must be short and direct. As language proficiency develops, the sentences can be lengthened to include subordinate clauses and other elements that increase the complexity of their construction and abstraction of their content.

Affective Qualities: Feelings/Emotions

Affective elements should be included, as children are very aware of the feelings and emotions that accompany the activities in their world. What they may not be able to do is to articulate them, or correctly attribute them—awareness of causation, subtlety of expression, understanding deeper motivations of those who are communicating with them, etc. We should look for opportunities to identify the feelings accompanying actions, describe the relationships of affect to action, and do so in simple and repeated ways:

> *The dog gets angry when you pull his tail. See how he shows his teeth and listen to his growling.*
>
> *I can see the sparkle in your eyes when we talk about going to the park to play on the swings.*
>
> *Grandma and Grandpa are very sad today. They are talking softly, and their eyes are sad. A good friend of theirs is very sick, and they are worried.*

This can be intensified by mimicry, when the soliloquy is accompanied by movement, facial expressions, and the like that amplify the feelings being verbalized.

Introducing Causal Relationships

At higher levels of soliloquy, these elements can be included:

- Identifying and including observations that introduce *teleological relationships*, or the goals of the actions being described:

> *When you shut the door I will not be able to see what you are doing.*

- The enunciation of intentions. Communication can begin to include feelings and emotions, describing these conditions relative to the context of what is being experienced. This focuses the child on the transcendence of language in relationships integrating the past, present, and future into personally experienced events.

    I am going to fill my glass with juice so I can drink it.

Introducing Relational Elements

The language experience can begin to help the learner make relationships among objects and events. A useful strategy is to point out common elements to be applied to a given object or event:

We drove in our car 2 hours to reach the beach. Last week we drove 3 hours when we went to visit our grandparents. The beach is closer to our house. Our grandparents live farther away, in a different direction.

SUMMING UP

In this chapter we have offered a number of direct suggestions regarding formulating the soliloquy to meet the developmental needs of the child and reflect meaningful aspects of language development, introducing dimensions of mental operations, through the application of MST—mediating the language activity so that it creates a platform for developing cognitive functions. The importance of this activity is grounded in the potential of the brain to be modified by experience (neuroplasticity).

Our language interactions with children are such a normal and a natural part of our lives that we often do not think about them, and—unless we have a good reason to do so—we do not systematically alter them. In this chapter we offer the reasons why we should and the ways to do it. In a later chapter we will discuss how to maintain and further advance these skills to help children develop linguistically and cognitively.

CHAPTER 7

Beyond Soliloquy
The Child's Response

In earlier chapters we have emphasized how the adult can facilitate and guide the introduction of language for the child. Here we ask the question: What should happen when the child engages in self-talk *and* begins to respond, expressing the language that has been stimulated?

As before, here we pay attention to a number of variables:

1. the nature and structure of the language to be conveyed,
2. the relationship between direct experience and linguistic elements related to it, and
3. the levels of awareness and activity that the child engages in.

As the child engages in self-talk, the adult observes and initially offers only limited responses to the child's verbalization, ultimately adjusting his or her subsequent verbalizations accordingly—offering further observations, in the form of adapted soliloquy. The child self-talks, and the adult observes this, leading to further adult response in the form of soliloquy that continues to be formulated and conveyed.

OBSERVING AND ASSESSING THE CHILD'S SELF-TALK

First of all, if the child has not spoken, or has very limited verbalization, the advent of his or her self-talk should be greeted with great enthusiasm—we should offer praise and other affirmation. For the adult who is observing and interacting with the child, the spontaneous self-talk will have a content and contextual process that can be very helpful in subsequent formulations of soliloquy. We pay attention to what the child is saying, how it is related to where the child is, and what the child is doing. The child's self-talk may be a consolidation of the exposure to the adult's soliloquy from an earlier time period, or from similar or different situations where overhearing is experienced. If it is highly imaginary, as it often is in young children, what is the nature of the image, and what kinds of needs or experiences is the self-talk related to? Is the child rehearsing some event that he or she will experience, such as going on a trip to a favorite place (a park) or a dreaded place (the dentist)? Is the child attempting to master a fear by talking to himself or herself about what needs to be confronted, such as crossing a busy street, or passing a fearsome animal (the big barking dog that lives nearby in the neighborhood)? As these and similar observations are made, the adult mediator can modify his or her utterances to focus or elaborate on various issues reflected in the child's soliloquy. Maintaining the essential criteria of soliloquy (that is, speaking in a way that does not demand either response or overt attention from the child), the focus and content of the adult's self-talk can serve to direct attention, reinforce feelings and awareness, and move the child's internal processes toward resolutions, feelings of competence, and mastery of new, unfamiliar, or emotionally threatening aspects of experience.

Another thing to observe in the child's self-talk is the structure of the language. Using some of the structural cues that we outlined in Chapter 4, the observing adult can pay attention to how the child is using language to elaborate on, differentiate, and describe the content of his or her talking. Mediation can then be directed toward aspects of what has been observed (see the parameters of MLE described in Chapter 2), oriented toward correcting or establishing missing or fragile linguistic functions, reinforcing or establishing modes of interaction, and developing the child's understanding and learning. Here is an example that shows some of these qualities:

> *You are afraid of the big dog. The dog is barking. The dog is barking because it is his way of talking. He cannot use words like you can . . . he can only bark. He is barking loudly because he is excited. You talk loudly when you are excited and happy. See . . . he is talking to you. He is telling you that someone is coming to the house. It is someone he is very glad to see. You can see his tail wagging. Even his barking sounds different. I think he is excited but happy! You will be happy to see this new person too. Your dog recognizes him and so will you.*

This can then be incorporated in an intentional and systematic way into the adult's subsequent verbal utterances, to provide models for structure. For example, if it is observed that the child does not use pronouns appropriately, or seldom uses descriptive adjectives, or omits referents, care can be taken to include them in adult utterances to model them and implicitly encourage imitation.

ENCOURAGING AND ELABORATING SELF-TALK ACTIVITY

Encouragement occurs when the adult does not interrupt the child's process, or act in any way critical or judgmental. Further encouragement occurs when the adult, knowing the content of the child's soliloquy, "arranges" for the child to be in a place where the situation encourages further or deeper inner processing. For example: A park that has dense foliage can be for the child a "tropical jungle" that can become an object for using the imagination—using a verbal modality. Climbing a tree or a rock formation can be a stimulant to project issues of fear, mastery, or fantasy. We are reminded of the taunt from the child who has climbed a steep hill, and once at the top calls down to the others, "I'm the king of the castle, and you're a dirty rascal" as he or she challenges others to try to match his feat of climbing.

We have observed children having watched an adventure film, and then going outdoors and projecting themselves into the scenes from the film, using their immediate experience, and both imitating the dialogue and embellishing the story in further dialogue. In these situations, a rich source of inner dialogue and self-talk expression is *created* and *experienced* by exposure to the film. Books and stories have the same potential.

In the young child's environment, there are many natural opportunities to engage in self-talk. Here are two very familiar and developmentally appropriate examples of self-talk in children, conforming to the conditions described above.

The Children's Tea Party: Preschool-age children love to have tea parties (even those who have never experienced such an event in their home or community lives). It appears that this is a universally related experience, where children join others (or engage in it as a solitary and fully projected experience) to simulate the event of meeting, sharing food and drink in a socially oriented interaction, and engaging in both the verbal and motor rituals associated with it. This becomes an opportunity to practice and experience verbal and social interactions—using language to connect to and explain the experience. Adults who may be offered opportunities to join the party are often expected not to talk, but to be passive participants in the event. It is the child who wants and needs to do the verbalizing; the adult is there to legitimize the experience. For the solitary child, adults can arrange such events frequently, including birthday celebrations (there is no reason why such children cannot have three or four birthday parties each year!), to increase children's experience with verbal and social interactions.

Imaginary Friends: At a similar age, children often acquire imaginary friends with whom they engage in extended dialogues. If these are listened to carefully, one can hear the child rehearsing events that they are anticipating, reminiscing about things that have happened to them, engaging in imaginary expositions, and the like. The second author's (Falik) younger son had a fantasy companion ("Jois") with whom he had an extended relationship (from the age of 3 to approximately 5). He would sit in the car on the way to and from various events—attending preschool, or going to family gatherings—discussing with his imaginary friend what he would be doing, what his plans were, the good or difficult things that were to be encountered, and so on. His parents would listen to the "conversation" but not intervene. We felt he knew we were listening, and wanted us to hear, but there was very little formal recognition of this friend or discussion of the content of the interaction. It is interesting to note that many years later, when he was in his 40s, he had a very keen memory of Jois, and even of some of the dialogues and the venues for these. In fact, he spontaneously analyzed the function of his friend in much the same way we have here. Jois was clearly an important aspect of his growing up and mastering his world. He also expressed his appreciation that his parents did not attempt to intervene conversationally, but "just listened."

These examples show the developmental and functional appropriateness of experiences such as these for the young child to master the linguistic aspects of his or her experience, and to give the adult an opportunity to look into a window on the child's verbal and experiential world.

MOVING AWAY FROM SELF-TALK

As valuable as self-talk is for the child, the adult mediator should consider when it is socially advisable to begin to convey to the child that some of what is being generated in the solitary modality can be transferred into the social realm and contribute to internalized thinking. Some children need to stay at the imaginary level longer than others—especially those who have special needs in the social development range, such as those in the autistic spectrum. For these children it is important to facilitate much imaginary processing, and be both accepting and patient regarding the positive outcomes for socialization that the child's self-talk offers.

However, for many children there comes a time when it is appropriate to say to them:

Don't just talk to yourself, talk to me. Tell others what you are talking about. They want to know what you are thinking about, what you know, what you want to know, etc.

This helps the child to move from externalization to internalization to socialization, communicating to others important aspects of experience. This is an important aspect of MLE, described earlier as the mediation of sharing behavior. It begins to move away from MST, but remains intimately related to it.

A HIERARCHY OF VERBAL INTERACTION: SOLILOQUY AND BEYOND

As we consider how to frame the soliloquy, how to observe, assess, and understand the child's self-talk, we are faced with the need to adapt and reformulate our verbal interactions in accordance with the changes we observe and the continuing developmental needs of the child, and to develop relevant goals that are identified and addressed through MLE. The perspective can be on both developmental tasks and the response to "disorders." We consider three levels of formulation and interaction: early soliloquy, guided soliloquy, and interactive conversation.

Early Soliloquy

In this phase the adult verbally describes actions and events, with *no expectation of the child's attention, and no grammatical framing that implies that a response is expected.* The language is enunciated descriptively, and is explicative of what is occurring. This is an important starting point, and is sustained over time and through many, many repetitions (remembering that in MLE we never simply repeat, but always add some type of variation that maintains the structure or general content but retains and repeats the rule and mediates transcendence—see Chapter 2). Most of the examples we have provided in earlier chapters are of this form. However, as time and exposure go on, and as some of the higher cognitive aspects of the verbalizations become possible and relevant, the soliloquy begins to include attributions of intention (*I am getting ready to eat the cookie*), anticipations of the future (*Soon there will be no more cookies on the plate*), and elaborations on the objects or events being depicted (*This chocolate chip cookie is especially delicious, and is my favorite. I am going to eat more than one!*).

Guided Soliloquy

The non-response expectation of the early phase of MST begins to transition into verbal utterances that, while they do not have a direct, explicit expectation of response, stimulate the child's thinking to formulate what may be an internal, implicit response. This level relates to developing the child's inner dialogue. It is accomplished by verbalizations that pose open-ended questions, and encourage speculative thinking. Examples of the former are *who, what, when, where, and why?* questions, posed as a verbalized manifestation of the adult's inner dialogue. Examples of these verbalizations would be: *Someone put the plate with the cookies on the table. I wonder who put them there. I wonder if I can eat them. I wonder if they taste as good as they look.* Notice that the utterances begin with *I wonder.* This is an excellent grammatical construction to encourage speculation, inference, and inner dialogue. These kinds of verbal formulations encourage, albeit indirectly and subtly, a more active engagement with the verbal content. This guiding relates to the mediator's bringing into the interaction elements that have been identified (from the observation and assessment of the child's needs and readiness) in a more systematic and focused way. This does not, interestingly enough, require great expertise from the mediator. Much of what is presented in this book can help in structuring what is verbalized, but the adult who is conversing with children, especially over time and across diverse contexts, often acquires a very natural and quite accurate sense of what the child needs and is ready for. However, remember our frequent caution and encouragement to go beyond what the learner appears immediately to be able to do, presenting challenges to which the learner can aspire, in this instance, providing grammatical constructions and exposure to content that is above the child's manifest levels of functioning, but also providing models to assimilate and eventually imitate.

Interactive Conversation

This is no longer MST, as it moves into a full verbal interaction with the child, capitalizing on and sometimes cycling back to earlier phases. The elements of MST, MLE, and the content of the interaction should reflect that which has gone before. As the encounter unfolds, the mediator acts as a guide, stimulator, and reflector of new accomplishments and past learning. The verbal interaction must be functional, gratifying, and effective in meeting the needs of the child. Mediation of feelings of competence, novelty, complexity and challenge, and sharing behavior are central to this phase of interaction. It is as important here to be as familiar with and facilitative of the stages in language development as it was for the earlier phases. Toward this end the taxonomy developed in Chapter 4 and the suggestions for implementing language formulations in Chapters 4 and 5 can be considered guidelines for continuing a focus on the sequence of speech and language proficiency that the mediator can work with, incorporating them into subsequent responses and verbal interactions. In this context, we continue to observe the child, present opportunities for language reception and expression, and facilitate learning through the mechanism of overhearing and the expectation of imitative processes.

An excellent illustration of this process is how the senior author's grandson, as a 5-year-old child, was encouraged to stand up at the Sabbath table, tell his assembled family about the Bible story of the week, and respond to questions from his family, who encouraged him to draw implications and meanings from the story. We also witnessed his indignation when, from time to time, this ritual was not followed. Typically he was given great appreciation for his accomplishment, and everyone assumed that it was his role in the family to make this presentation.

Similarly, in school, teachers will see children previously limited in language output now step into roles of narrator and interpreter of events, responding to additions and questions from peers and teachers.

CHAPTER 8

MST and Language Disorders

MST can be used with those experiencing various specifically identified speech and language disorders, including those that are developmental and those that follow various disabling conditions. As MST is directed toward language difficulties, it can play a role in overcoming, restoring, or enriching language skills and responses. This chapter reviews these disorders and considers MST in relation to them. As such, it will be helpful for parents who have children with speech and language disorders. For both specialists and laypersons, this chapter links MST to clinically diagnosed and labeled speech and language disorders.

APPLICATION OF MST TO LANGUAGE DISORDERS

The American Speech-Language-Hearing Association (ASHA) website lists a number of conditions that relate to speech and language difficulties—delays, disorders, and related conditions (see the ASHA website: www. asha.org). Our discussion will focus on those conditions that have relevance for the application of MST.

Speech Disorders

Childhood Apraxia of Speech describes motor speech disorders, where children have difficulty saying syllables, sounds, and words. Their brains have problems planning to move the appropriate body parts in the peribucal area. The child knows what to say but the brain has difficulty coordinating the necessary muscle movements. This disorder is also related to dysarthria, which is a weakness in muscle tone in the lips, jaw, and tongue.

Speech Sound Disorders are identified by their effects on processes of articulation and phonological awareness and production. We have addressed these latter conditions in several earlier chapters, as they relate to the structuring of the MST.

Orofacial **Myofunctional** **Disorders** describe conditions such as tongue-thrusting that interfere with correct pronunciation of some sounds (e.g., "sh," "ch").

Stuttering reflects problems with fluency of speech. They include repetitions, prolongation of speech sounds, and blockages of speech. When we describe bringing elements of prosody—the rhythm of speech—into MST, this is to address problems such as these.

Language Disorders

ASHA describes the effects of many *language-based learning disabilities* on the acquisition of speech and language processes. They also include *selective mutism* as a disorder in language, in which the child does not speak, even in the absence of any physiological or medical etiology.

Medical and Developmental Conditions

The ASHA taxonomy of disorders also lists *attention deficit/hyperactivity, autism, cleft lip and palate, right hemisphere brain injury,* and *traumatic brain injury* as conditions affecting speech and language development and production. Clearly the provision of MST can be an important intervention to overcome deficits and stimulate development and recovery. We encourage the reader to go to various readily accessible sites on the Internet, or to review the extensive literature on speech and language disorders to broaden understanding of the nature of the disorder and how MST can be productively applied.

For disorders such as these, without a necessarily specific relationship to diagnostic determinants, MST provides tools to expose individuals with specific language disorders to language models and to initiate productive interactions. We do not believe that etiology should be a barrier to mediational intervention. However, mediation needs to be directed toward a target for the intervention. In terms of etiology a language disorder may exist, in a general sense, due some of the following conditions:

- Known or unknown genetic syndromes (Down syndrome, Landau-Kleffner syndrome, Williams syndrome, Sotos syndrome, etc.).
- A brain injury or stroke.
- Negative environmental factors (poor linguistic context in the family, fetal alcohol syndrome, improper education, etc.).
- Unknown reasons—wherein the language disorder is intertwined

with certain behavioral disturbances (e.g., autism and specific language impairment).

In the current state, we acknowledge that more needs to be known about how to apply MST to the various disorders that we address in this chapter, although we know it can be helpful. We consider some of the variables contributing to this knowledge in the next chapter.

In terms of direction, a person might have trouble understanding others (*receptive language disorders*), or sharing thoughts, ideas, and feelings (*expressive language disorders*). When a large gap occurs between receptive language and expressive language (where either presents evidence of being dysfluent, fragmented, or underdeveloped), MST may have the potential to provide positive models and exposure to language, to reduce frustration levels, and to enrich and strengthen the individual's vocabulary and conceptual repertoire.

RESPONSES TO LANGUAGE DISORDERS

Here we summarize a number of things that have been presented in earlier chapters, but from the perspective of formulating MST to respond to language disorders. There are many natural and appropriate overlaps.

In terms of language structure, a disorder might affect:

- the prosody (the rhythm, stress, and intonation of speech)
- the phonology (sound system of any human language)
- the semantics (meaning)
- the morphology (structure of words—e.g., stems and suffixes)
- the syntax (structure of sentences)
- the pragmatics (interactional patterns) of the language of the individual
- the poverty of repertoire (culturally determined)—as an experiential factor and not due to pathology

We will briefly explain each of the above. They will have a differential presence in the child's developmental level, acquisition and proficiency, and response repertoire depending on the specific nature of the disorder.

Disorders of Prosody: *Aprosodia* is an acquired or developmental impairment in comprehending or generating the emotion conveyed in spoken language. Usually it means flat intonation and unusual voice quality, as is often present in cases of most genetic syndromes, traumatic brain injury (TBI), or cortical conditions such as cerebral palsy.

Disorders of Phonology: Children may have difficulty with the sounds of the language—they may find it difficult to recognize that two words begin with the same sound, or may place sounds in the wrong sequence. Or they might have poor articulation (*dyslalia*) or unintelligible speech. The reader should refer to our taxonomy related to articulation in Chapter 4, and adjust the activities from the recommended age levels to the child's particular level of need, working upward as proficiency is developed.

Disorders of Semantics: The child may find learning the meaning of words very difficult if there is *impaired lexical retrieval* (word-finding difficulties). One experiences this, for example, due to the condition of Wernicke's aphasia due to hemispheric lesions, or memory problems that may or may not have a cortical etiology. It is also a common disorder in certain genetic syndromes (e.g., Sotos syndrome or Down syndrome).

Disorders of Syntax: The child may struggle with words or parts of words and how they are put together to form phrases and sentences. For example, he or she may struggle to acquire particular morphemes, such as the third person singular, or may clearly utter single words, but struggle to link them together. Spatial localizers—"inside the house; into the house; out of the house, etc."—may be confused due to improper or underdeveloped spatial orientation in the proper linguistic construction of phrases and sentences—a very common cognitive delay that is immediately reflected in use of language.

Pragmatics: Sometimes it is difficult to master how words and sentences are used in different social and functional contexts. For example, the child may speak clearly and at length, but what they say seems irrelevant, poorly tracked to the content of what is occurring, or contextually incorrect. The child may be responding in a structurally correct manner but have poor articulation, and thus may not be intelligible to others. Inadequate answers on the part of the individual are often present in the case of autism or other cognitive delays.

Fluency Problems: Reduced verbal fluency or dysfluency as manifested in conditions of stammering or stuttering. Dysfluency is often connected to *word retrieval problems*, wherein the individual has the ideas and understanding, but cannot express them.

Poverty of Repertoire: There are some children who are not exposed to a rich or relevant vocabulary due to conditions of cultural discontinuity or economic poverty that restrict exposure and enriched experience. MST, offered by parents or teachers who are sensitized to the need (and potential), can use verbal exposure to overcome this limitation.

SPECIFIC LANGUAGE IMPAIRMENT (SLI): AN EXAMPLE OF THE EFFECTS OF A LANGUAGE DISORDER

This disorder is sometimes called *developmental dysphasia*. It illustrates that language is a system, and that a problem in one language area is likely to affect other areas, leaving the child with some impairment in vocabulary, grammar, and discourse skills. SLI is a peculiar type of language disorder that excludes those children who present with intellectual or physical disability, hearing loss, emotional problems, environmental deprivation, or sensorial problems. It is used to describe individuals (children and adults) whose *difficulties are with speech and language only*. Some typical difficulties are listed below:

1. the child seems to understand what is said, but people cannot understand what the child is trying to say;
2. the child speaks clearly and at length, but often fails to get the point of a conversation, making inappropriate comments and replies;
3. the child speaks clearly in single words, but has difficulties linking them together to make sentences, often leaving important words out; and/or
4. the child understands almost no spoken language and says only a few words.

Careful observation of the expressed language will indicate what needs to be paid attention to in the construction of the soliloquy—bringing in models that link objects to action; adding accurate agreement of tense, number, and the like—indicating that the nature of the language difficulties as we summarized them above are largely, but not exclusively, in the syntactical area. The producer of the soliloquy can craft verbalizations to correct and model accurate and appropriate constructions. Children with SLI usually begin talking late. Many will have limited vocabulary and produce only short utterances at 3 and 4 years of age. Moreover, children with SLI may have striking differences in what they are and are not able to say or understand. Language difficulties range from those who understand almost no spoken language and can say very few words, to those who talk at length but irrelevantly. Given what we have presented in earlier chapters, one can see important benefits of using MST to address various types of language disorders.

Despite the variety of causes of conditions, MST has the potential to provide children and others in need with more adequate models of conceptualizing, constructing, and expressing language, under conditions of stimulation and acceptance. MST does not do everything that is needed to overcome disability, but can—in conjunction with other interventions—be a major help.

CHAPTER 9

Language Development, Cognitive Development, and Social Development

Overcoming Developmental Delay

In this chapter we tell the story of Elchanan, the son of Rafi Feuerstein and grandson of Reuven Feuerstein. For this reason we tell it in the first person, in the words of his father. Elchanan's experience illustrates the role of MST in his development, starting with pre-language and moving into language and related social and academically oriented mediation.

Elchanan was born 22 years ago with Down syndrome. Today he is a well-groomed young man who has completed his required studies from elementary school to high school in a regular school and has taken and passed a good part of the required national secondary school completion certification tests. Elchanan is about to be accepted into the Israeli Army as a volunteer, and he is planning his future life—above all, his wish is to be married and to raise a family.

Due to his excellent language functioning and thinking, during his high school years he became known as the "class philosopher" to whom other students came to discuss questions of ethics and morals in their Biblical studies.

THE BEGINNINGS

How did this linguistic ability of Elchanan's occur? We applied the soliloquy method almost from the beginning of his development.

The soliloquy method gives the parent a huge advantage. This is an *interactive* relationship. Every natural encounter of the parent with the child becomes an opportunity for mediation and in our case, for soliloquy. Thus, we had to transform ourselves into *mediating parents*. We learned to exploit everyday situations in order to advance his language. This does not mean to say that at a later age Elchanan did not notice that he was receiving mediation more than his siblings, and at times did not like this. He would say to us, from time to time, when he was about 15: "Stop educating me!" At various times in his growing years, his reaction to the large degree of mediation that he needed required us to search for others to mediate him—bringing a neutral and fresh energy and some technical skills that we did not possess, and giving us options to continue our parental mediation.

THE INTENTION

The Pre-Linguistic Phase

The environment surrounding Elchanan, as with any baby or child, was varied and rich. The addition of verbal stimuli at this stage in the child's environment while he or she is engaged in actual activity is liable to be perceptually peripheral and undifferentiated from all of the other sensory input. Thus the first task of establishing soliloquy is to stimulate the child's natural and innate capacity to imitate both sounds and gestures that are provided in his or her immediate environment. We knew that we needed to penetrate our child's cognitive system with an awareness of several critical pre-verbal aspects of later speech. To this end, we shaped the stimuli for Elchanan.

During the first weeks of Elchanan's life we held his head at a distance of about 16 inches from us so that he would maintain eye contact. Speech from too great a distance was liable not to be heard or absorbed. We raised the level of our voices in order to overcome competing environmental noises, and to capture his attention.

All of us who became his mediators—his parents, older siblings, and various extended family members—engaged in a systematic and repeated interaction. We held him in such a way that his face was directed toward the mediator, moving his head slightly to restore contact if his gaze shifted away. Then we exaggerated the shape of our mouths, forming and emitting sounds: first, *bah, bah, bah* (widening and narrowing the lips, but with open mouth), then *boo, boo, boo* (with the lips formed into a circular shape), and then *bo, bo, bo* (with the lips in an exaggerated circular shape and the lips protruding and extended outward). This was done repeatedly, for several minutes at a time, over extended time periods, eventually widening and varying the sounds and shaping of the mouth. Our goal was to reinforce the response of his peribucal, or mouth, muscles. Within a relatively short time, we observed Elchanan anticipating the event, starting to shape his mouth in response to his observations—even as he was picked up and placed in position. He began to mimic the mouth movements of the adult as the sounds were being produced. We also observed changes in the focusing of his gaze, becoming more consistent over increasingly longer time spans. This was completely consistent with Professor Feuerstein's clinical experience and research on the role of stimulation as described above on the number of repetitions needed to elicit the behaviors described. It has been shown that children need approximately 90 repetitions with the first sounds, going down to 70, and eventually 30, with continued repetitions and sequencing of exposure. Elchanan got many more!

Relatively soon, this behavior generalized into Elchanan paying attention to other individuals emitting sounds. He began looking around to find the sources of sounds in his environment, watching the faces of those speaking, and imitating the motor facial movements associated with the sounds he heard. Around this time he also began to protrude his tongue as an imitative response to the mediators' stimulation. This progression, so important for Elchanan's subsequent linguistic development, and consistent with well-established research findings, was what needed to be done to stimulate and involve the movements that are related to speech production, and is often the first stage in the process of MST.

Early Language Experience

In later infancy, we watched for indications of attention, even very fleeting ones, and began to insert relevant speech, whether or not his attention was sustained. For example, when Elchanan asked for a snack (his word for this was "Bamba"), he would screw up his face and half shout/half cry in the direction of his mother who was holding the bag, while stretching his hand toward her. Elchanan was focused on his need. His mother would say to him: "Say, please," and repeat this several times. And after placing the snack in his hand she would say to him: "Thank you . . . thank you . . . thank you," several times. She repeated the name "Bamba" (exaggerating the second syllable) to him a number of times.

This illustrates how natural situations, such as when the child asks his parents for food or a drink, games or books, is a common event, and can be exploited for later linguistic (and attention) gain. From the perspective of language development, the systematic exploitation of events of this kind, accompanied by appropriate speech on our part, helped Elchanan learn that a connection existed between speech and behavior and to equip him with a relevant vocabulary.

When we dressed Elchanan and he allowed us to take his hand and insert it into the shirt or sweater sleeve, this too was an "exploitable" situation, generally permitting attention. Here too we accompanied our actions with various descriptive terms and labels: the names of limbs (*hand, leg, arm, foot*, etc.), or spatial terms such as *right hand, left hand, right foot*, and *left foot*. In all these examples we exploited the relative attentiveness of Elchanan in order to accompany the action with speech. In those activities in which Elchanan was engaged and focused, the accompanying speech had an important role—even when his attention wasn't focused on our faces and our speech. The accompanying and echoing speech formed part of the stimulus penetrating into him. We would raise our voices to a level that would capture his attention, accompanied by behavioral manipulations such as putting him in our hands, and bodily gestures in order to assure our presence in the process.

SOME OBSERVATIONS ON THE PROCESS TO THIS POINT

The Focus

We understood fairly quickly that beyond the sentences that we spoke to Elchanan and that were accompanied by his and our actions, we should select some key words to focus on during the course of the week. Thus, our refrigerator turned into a crowded notice board on which we hung two or three "key words" for each week. We worked according to word "families" (categories). For a certain period we focused on colors and then on directions (*up, down, right, left*, etc.), and so on. We observed that the constant repetition of the same words produced the hoped-for results—in alertness, and the beginning of formulation of words. We also took care to repeat previous words over and over in order to preserve them. And, of course, the selected words (and concepts) of the week were embedded in full sentences. But we emphasized the words and repeated them several times within the same sentence. One example: *Elchanan is playing with the blue cube. Blue, blue, the blue cube, blue. So beautiful.* An important note here . . . the words and sentences are produced very early, and well before a child can produce or reproduce comparable language.

The Quantity

The intentionality of the process also finds expression in the intensity of the stimulus. The speech has to be present as much as possible. I see many parents who practically do not speak to their special needs child. I fully understand them. It is hard to talk when the child does not respond. There is an element of expectation and the satisfaction of verbal interaction with one's child that does not occur, which we (as Elchanan's parents) and many other parents must work hard to overcome. There is an internal change in the role that we are used to assigning to language. For us language is an interactive medium, the means of interpersonal communication. At this point, it was necessary to speak with someone without knowing whether he understood us at all. I overcame this obstacle by creating a habit—a behavioral pattern that bypassed consciousness. When it became a habit it did not consume the energy of deliberation, making a decision, or harnessing resources of will. At first this was hard. But the more we repeated this behavior it became increasingly easy. It became a habit that helped us to speak a lot to our child. The constant and large amount of speech is one of the foundations of the MST method, and this is what in the final analysis penetrates into the child and teaches him that language and speech are an inseparable part of our world of action.

The amount of language teaches the child that language reflects every action or object that exists in our world. Language is like a giant mirror that gives expression to almost everything; language is relevant and significant in every event and every thing. To this end we were careful as parents not to give in to Elchanan, not to take the easy way and simply give him what he wanted and needed. Whenever he would ask something of us we demanded speech, or we modeled the relevant linguistic construction, and verbalized what could or should accompany the action. The message to the child had to be clear—that speech was the central channel of communication between us.

Transmission (Transcendence) in Mediation

This brings an expansive quality to the linguistic experience for the child. If his T-shirt was blue, he needed to know that the color was not unique to just this T-shirt, but that many other objects—some similar to his shirt and many others that were quite different—also are the color blue. And the color can be searched for, differentiated (shades of color), and given functional meaning (the blue color of police officers' uniforms is so that people will recognize them when they are needed). We told him when we dressed him in the morning: *Put on the blue shirt, the blue. And look at the sky outside* (turning his head to the window), *it's blue, the sky is blue. And the carpet is also blue, blue . . .* This was carried on in the situation itself, and in other contexts during the day, and thus extended in relation to as many other nouns and verbs as possible. We stressed their varied appearance in order to differentiate them from known and prominent objects. Our goal (combining both intentionality and transcendence) was to transmit the perception of the language as generic, as lacking a specific content, and as belonging in principle to a wide range of objects. We also created linguistic flexibility in the opposite direction (see our discussion of syntax in Chapter 4). One can say, *the shirt is blue,* and one may also say, *the color of the shirt is blue.* This means that we also tried to reach a world of higher concepts such as color, form, number, direction, etc., and Elchanan had to get used to varied levels of concretization of the linguistic description (again, see our discussion of linguistic elements such as semantics, syntax, and pragmatics in Chapter 4). Thus, for instance, we could say to him: *The shirt is blue* or, *the garment is blue.* Further, we could relate to other characteristics of the shirt: *the shirt is beautiful* or, *the shirt has short sleeves.* This meant that the shirt had many descriptions. It had color, form, and a certain role. This meant that every object had more than one potential description. All these form part of the creation of a flexible structure of language.

Synergy

The advantage of the family environment is that as parents we are not alone in this endeavor, but can call upon the child's siblings. Calling upon the child's siblings has a number of advantages: (1) There is more mediation in general, and soliloquy in particular, because there are more potential mediators; (2) There comes a time when the growing child begins the separation process, minimizing the influence of his parents, or at least reducing their presence. This happened with Elchanan. When he was about 15 he would say to me: "Stop educating me. Enough, I've grown up, you have educated me enough." The great amount of mediation that we gave him as parents needed to be reframed and delivered differently if it was to be effective. Consequently, decentralization (in the sense of division—bringing more people as mediators into his life) of the mediation among more persons has great significance.

How does one turn the child's siblings into effective soliloquy mediators? In our case there were two quite distinct stages. Elchanan is our second child, and after him six more brothers and sisters were born, in quite close sequence. Therefore, we were able to mediate to his younger brothers the process of soliloquy (both overtly and through modeling) so that it also included him, although without pressuring him with excessive mediation, which was liable to prevent him from cooperating with us. In the area of language development, this is a critical dimension. The inclusion of his siblings had an additional benefit. Elchanan gained multiple models. He learned, for example, how to carry on a correct dialogue.

Imitation

We began from the age of 2 weeks to work on Elchanan's imitative ability. To this end, the senior author (Elchanan's grandfather, Professor Reuven) would arrive at his grandson's home and for about an hour each day would hold the tender infant in his arms, at a distance of about 16 inches from his face, as we described. It was amazing to see Elchanan's face at the age of 2 or 3 weeks, beginning to screw up his face and really imitate the look on the face of his mediating grandfather. Others in the family observed the grandfather and began to imitate him in reproducing the mediation for Elchanan.

At a certain stage we began to work on words. And then, every time we said a word, we broke it up into syllables: *a-ba* (father), *i-ma* (mother), *sha-lom*. Each syllable was stressed, clearly articulated, and isolated from the one next to it. We also stressed the first syllable in a low tone of voice, whereas the last syllable we enunciated in a loud voice. It was important for us to emphasize the start of the word and its ending in order to prevent Elchanan from swallowing the ends or beginnings of words. The division into syllables was exploited not only to help him to absorb this or that word. This division was designed to give him a working method for acquiring longer and more complicated words. He learned through this aspect of the enunciation to break words into syllables and to master longer words with multiple syllables. I remember that when Elchanan was 5, and half-seriously and half-jokingly I said to him, Say "university" (a five-syllable word), Elchanan succeeded and spontaneously broke up the word into syllables. This meant that Elchanan not only created a rich vocabulary, but also learned how to teach words to himself and to exploit spontaneously and independently the spoken environment surrounding him.

Some Emotional Aspects of Soliloquy

Elchanan was 2 years old and was sitting on my knee in the living room of our home. I began to count with him to ten. This was something new that I had not yet tried with him. As I would start to say each number, Elchanan completed it. I now realized that Elchanan could count to ten. But I had not consciously taught this in a systematic or (from my perspective) purposeful manner. When I checked to find out who had taught him, it turned out that nobody had. I realized that Elchanan had become an independent learner. The significance of this change was far-reaching for me. I understood that my son with Down syndrome was a clever child and that, with G-d's help, he had a future. This certainly enhanced my optimism, courage, and engagement with his learning potential.

EVENTUALLY . . . WITHOUT LIMITS OR BOUNDARIES

By the age of 3, Elchanan possessed a vocabulary of hundreds of words. And he spoke in clear and well-constructed sentences. But all these achievements did not set our minds at rest. Elchanan would sit down on the rug, holding a cord or long electric cable, wave it and create with it snake-like, winding movements, simultaneously creating word-chains as long as the cord itself, interconnected associatively. And thus he could sit for a whole hour waving the long cord and singing as he did so an endless chain of words, as if totally cut off from the external environment, and it was very difficult to get him to abandon this activity.

We were very worried by this behavior. It was as if our child had gone completely out of control. The one who voiced a very clear opinion, based on his very rich experience, was his grandfather, the senior author of this book. He told us:

> Don't worry, this is a very important stage in the linguistic development of Elchanan. For several reasons: first, he is repeating the words he has learned. His repetition is essential in order to ensure the internalizing of the many words he has acquired; secondly, he is using them in a very flexible way. The associative connection he creates between the words, in a very irregular way, builds the infrastructure for the creative use of the language.

One of the lessons we drew as young parents was that human development is not linear and that it is more reminiscent of a dialectical track in which a certain "thesis" takes control of the child's soul in an extreme manner and is then hidden by opposing behavior (antithesis). And in the end it balances out.

LATER DEVELOPMENT

This pattern of Elchanan's linguistic (and social and cognitive) development was repeated in several stages as he grew chronologically. Between the ages of 9 and 15 he would congratulate the family members on their birthdays. At the family ceremony Elchanan would utter words of congratulation characterized by four things: they were always moving since it was clear that they came from the depth of his heart; they were very long; they were very associative and moved from topic to topic with no defined logical structure, but with a striking associative connection; and they were very rich in terms of vocabulary and ideas. As time passed, and as these family rituals were repeated, Elchanan's contributions became more restrained, and he became more precise in his language. He congratulated briefly. The linguistic richness and ideological richness vanished. Elchanan had become almost too boring and exact. I remember that one of my children suddenly exclaimed with regret: "*What happened to Elchanan's rich and vibrant congratulations?*" However, Elchanan developed into a fine public speaker—the speech he made at the end-of-year ceremony in his school, in front of all the parents, I shall never forget. His speech was rich, to the point, fluent, wise, and amusing.

In his teens Elchanan developed a habit of speaking to himself (this was described briefly in Chapter 5). He would construct for himself an imaginary world that he called "a band," which was populated by many friends, each of whom had a role and a character of his own. Elchanan would shut himself away for hours and organize the band's life. This included meetings and varied events. Listening to the loud words of Elchanan in those days revealed an extremely rich vocabulary and a rich and creative imagination. We parents, worried by the virtual world that Elchanan appeared to be living in, needed guidance. Again, his grandfather, as was his wont, knew how to calm and reassure us, explaining that this was the way in which Elchanan internalized the language and the principles of social life. In the long term we saw to what extent there appear to be learning mechanisms that assume a kind of extreme outward expression but that serve well-defined aims, directed at internalizing what has been learned and developing the ability to use it with great flexibility.

THE BROADER ENVIRONMENT

Elchanan's verbal development was stimulated by the normal environment that he participated in from early childhood. Elchanan learned in regular kindergartens and classes. It had a tremendous impact on his personal behavior and verbal development. Regular environments exposed Elchanan to normative language in all its forms: vocabulary, syntax, the regular pragmatics of the language, the cultural and individual richness expressed in language, and the role of language in replacing behavior. Dozens of hours of speech therapy could not compare with the mediating power that he was exposed to in his regular classes, youth groups, and the like.

At certain points in his development Elchanan needed someone to consolidate his academic learning and maintain his integration in normal classrooms. We found, for short periods of time, skilled and caring individuals who could support and mediate him in this regard, and eventually enable him to function successfully and comfortably.

In his normative environment Elchanan learned to listen to his peers because his learning in class depended upon this listening—when the teacher spoke to the class she was speaking to him as well. Elchanan learned that when the teacher told the pupils to take out a certain book *he* must do so, even though she had not addressed him personally. Elchanan had to learn the nature of a precise instruction in a basketball game with his classmates, by contrast with an instruction on the worksheet given to him for homework. He had to listen to a text that somebody read and take from it sufficient hints in order to discover the reader's place in the text. For example, during prayers in the synagogue, recited from a written text in the prayer book, he had to find the congregation's place in the text before him.

Another factor was the *environmental* quality of his family and community culture—leading to an affinity for reading. Elchanan completed the reading of an ancient Hebrew legal codex (written about 1,800 years ago) 24 times, reading thousands of pages word for word aloud in the process. At the beginning we did not assume that his level of understanding was high or even minimal. This is a difficult text for any student or reader, and even the well-versed student has to refer to commentators in order to fully understand what he is reading. Nonetheless, his vocabulary grew remarkably, and the level of his understanding, at least generally, improved. Today, at the age of 22 (he began when he was 13) he is able to say more or less where almost any major topic he is asked about is located. His ability to develop and to try to understand what he is reading and even hearing has improved immeasurably following this intensive and prolonged reading. The lesson here: Exposure to the language, even if it is not immediately understood by the child, contributes in the medium and long terms.

Television presented a dilemma. We did not wish to raise our children under what we considered to be the addictive influence of a culture not always of a high standard and contrary to many of our values. But we understood that the verbal simulation to which he was exposed had to be intensified. So we had a television, but controlled the input. We exposed Elchanan to animated films that he watched a good deal. This process began when Elchanan was 6. To our surprise, Elchanan began to say the dialogue of his favorite films along with his favorite characters. At first he tried to keep up with their flow of words. Within a short time he learned the dialogues of dozens of scripts. He knew all the songs, along with the facial expressions of the heroes and their gestures, and he imitated these along with the action on the screen. But above all, his language was enriched within a short time by many new words, and also by the ability to form sentences.

MST IN ADULTHOOD

Does MST still have a place in adulthood? For Elchanan and all other adults, the goals must be changed. The emphasis on vocabulary enrichment can be reduced. What then is the role of MST for adults?

One brief example: from the time Elchanan was 18, I began to exploit the time in which I drove him in the car. I began to include in our journey together the creation of a map (conceptual/verbal) of the road we were traveling on, thereby attempting to create in him a developed system of spatial attribution. This is how I did it: as I drove the car on the road leading out of the neighborhood I would ask Elchanan to anticipate and guide me as to where to turn. At the beginning I would cue him, *where shall we turn from the junction . . . We will turn left in the direction of the gas station. And where will we get to at the end of the road that goes upward?* As he internalized these directions, I would add details and the scope of anticipation until we had an extensive travel planning dialogue occurring. What was my goal with this MST? I wanted to use this time to develop Elchanan's processing. And, more concretely, I wanted to develop in him the skill of creating a mental map. I wanted to develop the cognitive ability to: (1) visualize space in the form of verbal representations, and (2) be able to plan his route on the basis of these internalized mental maps.

The aim of MST here, and in many other available examples, is to reflect and to open him to a wider, more complex, and both internally and externally meaningful reality in the world around him, to materialize his potential to be a full participant in his community and society.

A FINAL REFLECTION

We have included our family and personal experience with Elchanan because it portrays the full spectrum of language development and its effect on not only his verbal skills but also his social and cognitive development. Ultimately, these aspects must be provided and integrated. They must be prepared for, provided repeatedly and systematically. By systematically we mean that adjustments must be made. We got discouraged. We often did not understand the meaning of his behaviors, or misjudged their functions and progressions. We would get fatigued or impatient for more or faster change.

We had to have help, and that we received from his grandfather (the senior author of this book—within our family and as our mentor). We mention this last point because we know that often outside help is required—to maintain focus, encourage and sustain our efforts, and give us the courage and purpose to go on, but importantly, to also see the positive changes that occur, and to use them for further responding. These are the enduring themes of this book—as we develop and implement MST.

CHAPTER 10

Applying MST to Different Needs

Brief Case Studies

The case studies in this chapter illustrate the ways in which MST is presented to children and its effect on changing them. They are cases where MST was first used by therapists, who then involved parents and others in the implementation of the approach. We present them to give you a picture of how MST is done by people very familiar with it, showing their decisions about how and when to use it, and their innovations and outcomes. We believe that even if you are a "non-professional" in the language field (parent, teacher, caretaker), you can gain both insight and encouragement from these descriptions, further understand the theory and practices, and will optimistically be willing to try it out—in the context of your child's needs and your relationship with him or her. As you read the cases think about the rationale and component elements that we have described in earlier chapters of this book.

We have included the details of how the various elements were put into place, and how they were sequenced, repeated, developed, and reinforced. In addition to how MST was implemented, we will offer some of the dynamics of the case and underlying reasons for what was done and how it was done. We have selected cases illustrating differing applications and differing types of children and learners with whom MST was utilized.

Case 1: Donald—
MST as Early Intervention

Donald was 4 years old and was not speaking. His therapist decided to use MST to stimulate his language, and do so in a way that his mother could observe and eventually emulate in her daily interactions with the child. In initial sessions Donald did not make eye contact, sat on his mother's lap, and did not seem focused or engaged with the stimuli surrounding him.

The therapist decided to start the therapeutic intervention in a very gentle way, interacting with the mother and the child using MST. She did not send the mother from the room, but started applying the MST approach by producing "observational monologues," phrased in the first person singular, and without the implication (direct or indirect) that any response from the child was expected or desired.

Early Phase

In the first phase (for about 2 weeks) the therapist did not attempt to initiate eye contact with Donald, just looked out of the window or at the table, not requiring any response or reaction from him. In terms of content, she systematically planned the therapeutic scene: in the first part of the session she used a "reporting technique," describing the room, its qualities, the placement of furniture, etc., and the people in it (the bold words reflecting vocal emphasis):

> *Oh, there are three **people** in this room! I can see your **mother** sitting on a chair. I can see a little boy as well. **The boy** is sitting on his mother's lap. And the third person is **me**. My name is Agatha. **Mother, boy,** and **Agatha. Barbara, Donald,** and **Agatha.** They are in the room.*

This was accompanied by gestures—exaggerated pointing to each person referred to, with energy and repetition.

In this interchange, the communication is clear but the response mode was "passive." The therapist used her voice to emphasize certain elements—in this case the people in the environment. This was repeated numerous times, and returned to later in the therapy, even after more advanced stages were experienced.

We assume that the child is listening, using the mechanism of *overheard language*, although not necessarily overtly paying attention. It is important to move slowly in the first phase.

As the therapist sensed that the protagonists were ready and accepting, the intensity and focus was increased. This required the therapist's observation and facility with techniques and an understanding of how to elicit responses consistent with language and concept development.

The Next Phase

The therapist introduced wooden animal puzzles and began to imitate animal voices. She backed up the linguistic input with visual pictures (a wooden sheep or cat, for instance)—but very slowly, in a cadence and with restricted content, putting emphasis on the sound the animal makes.

She often substituted the name of the animal with the voice it produces (*bow-wow* for dog; *ney-ney* for horse, etc.).

In terms of language structure the therapist began to introduce nouns (*horse, cat, dog*, etc.) at this point. The therapist was constantly talking to herself but kept the boy's needs in her mind: she used *simple syntactic structures*, much *repetition*, and *talked slowly* (again accompanying her speech with exaggerated gestures).

> *I am holding a **horse** in my hands. The **horse** is an animal. The horse says neey, neey, neey.*

Sometimes she initiated simple structured plays with the horses:

> *I hear one of the horses can speak. This **horse** says: I am a **horse**. I like eating **apples, apples, apples**. What is your name* [talking to the other horse]? *I like other **animals** as well. My favorite animal is **ladybug**. **La'dy-bug** has a black dot on its back. **la-la-la-la-ladybug**.*

Notice that in spite of a very active performance on the part of the therapist, there was no expectation of a response from Donald or his mother. It remained a soliloquy! The therapist did not make her language utterances contingent upon whether the child responded.

The therapist used her voice very consciously and systematically, varying intonation—raising/falling, then falling, sometimes just raising intonation in an exaggerated way when enunciating the names of people or animals or food. She artificially put the stress on the second or third syllable (e.g., *mo-ther, la-dy-bug, lady-bug*) of the nouns. The therapist was playing with the melody of words . . . using the musicality of the language. She hoped that this would interest Donald, that he would be attracted by the objects themselves, the content of the speech to which he was being exposed, and the internalized language structures that were presumed to be there in his awareness. His reactions signaled that he was, in fact, paying attention. When he noticed that the therapist used a strange or unexpected intonation, not really used in the given language, and when he was exposed to the very strange stress patterns, he raised his eyebrows (perhaps wondering what this strange thing wanted to be), and increased his focus.

The Third Phase

In the next phase (lasting about another 2 weeks) the therapist asked the mother to move with Donald and sit in a corner of the room, away from the table at which they had been working in the previous sessions. She continued her first person singular monologues, however. In this and subsequent sessions, after the first few minutes, Donald spontaneously left his mother's lap and began to come closer to the table, changing his proximity and maintaining eye contact. He eventually stood up holding the edge of the therapist's table, looking into the therapist's face as she spoke. He watched the therapist's lips, and alternatively looked at the toys on the table that she was speaking about.

In terms of content the therapist was using other members of different categories (vehicles, activities, furniture, etc.) related but somewhat beyond the visible toys on the table—starting to introduce a representational element. In terms of structure she started to increase the length of utterances and combined the different names of the objects (nouns)—for example, *the car and the motorbike, the bed and the chair, the tiger and the rabbit.*

A Further Phase

The next change in Donald's responding occurred when he took an object from the therapist's hands and started imitating human speech. Some of the words were quite similar to the proper words. In this fourth phase of the intervention, after the first month of therapy, the therapist increased the complexity of her verbal utterances. Stress was put on verbs and actions, combined with the nouns of the first two phases.

> *I am sitting at the table. Like last time we were together. Also **Barbara** is **sitting**. **Mother** is **sitting** in the other corner of the room.*

Also, spatial localizers (e.g., *on, on top of, in, inside,* etc.) were emphasized.

Here, the therapist observed changes in the child's spontaneous responding and increased the complexity of the language, beginning to move beyond soliloquy by encouraging and responding to the child's responses. Little direct notice was made of the child's movement away from the mother, so as not to change the focus of the verbal interaction. It was clear that the child was focusing on the language produced by the therapist, and starting some initial social contacts related to it. These were considered important changes.

The Last Phase of the MST

In the final phase of the intervention the therapist started to include questions in the soliloquy (with certain words receiving vocal emphasis):

Again I can see three people in my room. Why is it that there are only three people in this room? Why is it that only Barbara, Donald, and Agatha are here? Probably it is because Peter is at work. Where is my friend, Peter? He is at work . . .

Questions are the hardest in terms of syntactic structures, and raise the complexity of the language significantly. Donald did not directly respond, but indicated by eye contact, the physical movement of looking at the named figures in the sentence, and such that he was listening, and it was making sense.

Affecting the Parents: Donald's mother had observed each session. After the first several sessions, the therapist took a few minutes at the conclusion to explain to the mother what she was doing and why she was doing it. The goal was to gently and slowly expose her to the theory and practical application of MST. Moreover, Donald's mother was given the opportunity to ask questions, plan ways in which she could extend and adapt her language for him, and request help from the therapist (*how should I say that, what should I respond when he says . . .*). The therapist observed the mother spontaneously producing short soliloquies as she entered and left the therapy sessions. This encouraged the therapist to suggest that she (the mother) and the father start to "talk to themselves" at home and in shared activities in the presence of Donald.

Eventually, toward the latter phases of the therapy with Donald, his mother appeared amenable to longer discussions about how real-life opportunities were rich in content and she was encouraged to speak about her feelings in the house to depict the actual activities they were doing, and to bring soliloquy into many social situations.

Progress in Language Acquisition: Donald's language started to evolve after about the first month of exposure to MST. In the beginning his mother counted 11 words (all nouns), then 2 weeks later he had 50. By the seventh week he was saying sentences like *Barba' (his mother) is working*. After the eighth week he was picking up about five or six new words each day. His mother was engaged in the process by being asked to keep track and record Donald's new words. In this way she was in some control of the changing process, and could attest to his progress. The active therapy was terminated, but the mother came in approximately every 3 weeks to report progress, discuss strategies to sustain Donald's language development, and get encouragement and support.

The reader may view the above depiction of actions and progress as unrealistically positive. Can things really develop so rapidly? As we have worked with therapists, parents, and care providers on early versions of the MST approach, we are getting feedback that such rapid and structurally meaningful changes are not unusual. The next cases we describe offer further evidence for this!

Case 2: Amy—
A 10-Year-Old Girl Diagnosed as Autistic

Amy was diagnosed as autistic. She was in cognitive/behavioral therapy for almost 4 years. At the outset of the intervention reported here, in a different therapeutic encounter, she spoke in very short, simple sentences and did not maintain eye contact. She had been home-schooled by her parents. The treatment plan included exposure to both the Feuerstein Instrumental Enrichment (FIE) program (Feuerstein & Hoffman, 1994) and MST. She had a number of functional deficiencies: among them, blurred and sweeping perception, poor eye/hand coordination, poor recognition of the alphabet and sight words, limited use of prepositions, an inability to do simple mathematical operations, and very limited spontaneous speech.

Initially, Amy's deficiencies were addressed using the FIE tools, and positive results were obtained after a lot of hard work, tears, and frustration. She would show improvement and then regress, show good response and then throw a tantrum on other days. It was decided to bring MST into the treatment plan, and the therapists experimented with different ways of using the mediated soliloquy activities to address various aspects of her functioning, with much innovation and consideration of alternatives and her responses.

In this case study, we will describe in some detail the way in which MST was directed toward several different aspects of Amy's behavioral development.

Language Development

One example is how soliloquy was used to stimulate the learning of prepositions. A goal was formulated to teach Amy the concept of the word *on*. The verbal interaction that was generated (see below) was recorded by a digital voice recorder so that she could listen to it many times and in the presence of different adults. Her parents played it for her at different times of the day when she was in the house and engaged in quiet play activities. The use of a recorder represents an innovation in constructing MST, responding to several conditions in Amy and her family's life. The therapists felt that it offered several advantages that will be described in the text that follows. Here is the script, which was repeated with variations in the treatment over a number of sessions:

> *The apple is on the table. Is the apple under the table? No, the apple is not under the table, the apple is on the table.*
>
> *Is the apple beside the table? No, the apple is not beside the table, the apple is on the table.*
>
> *Is the apple on the table? Yes, the apple is on the table.*
>
> *Is the apple touching the surface of the table? Yes, the apple is touching the surface of the table. On means the apple must touch the surface of the table.*
>
> *Is the apple above the surface of the table? No, the apple is not above the surface of the table. On means the apple must touch the surface of the table.*
>
> *Is the apple supported by the surface of the table? Yes, the apple is supported by the surface of the table. On means the apple must be supported by the surface of the table.*
>
> *Is the apple being crushed by the surface of the table? No, the apple is not being crushed by the surface of the table. On means the apple must be supported by the surface of the table, not being crushed.*
>
> *Is the apple being squeezed by the surface of the table? No, the apple is not being squeezed by the surface of the table. On means the apple must be supported by the surface of the table, not being squeezed.*

The above script was presented as a monologue, with the therapist both asking and answering the questions. The goal here (and throughout) is to create 5–10 minute interactions that were recorded to be played back later at home and in the presence of the parents and others in the family. The strategy of recording the interactions, with the mother observing, and then encouraging the mother to play it back for her at different times during the day at home, was effective. It gave the mother a sense of being active and successful in the treatment, and the mother began to initiate other soliloquies using the taped interaction as a model. Notice also that the monologue introduced new vocabulary and concepts (e.g., *crushed, squeezed*) along with the focus on the prepositions that was the main goal.

Interestingly, Amy's mother had tried for many years to teach her various linguistic constructions. At the outset of treatment, before using the MST method, the therapist also tried to effect changes in language, but with limited success. With the infusion of soliloquy, using the script described above, within a relatively short time span, Amy mastered eight prepositions.

Reading

The MST method was used in reading instruction. In this example, Amy was taught to differentiate *here* and *her*.

Is this word here? Yes, this word is here.
  Is this word her? No, this word is not her, this word is here.
  Can we read this word as her? No, we cannot read this word as her.
This word is here.
  Can we read this word as here? Yes, we can read this word as here.
  Do we read h-e-r-e (spelled) as her? No, we don't read h-e-r-e as her.
  H-e-r-e is read as here. Do we read h-e-r-e as here? Yes, we read h-e-r-e
as here.

The monologue was repeated in the therapy session, was recorded, and Amy listened to the recording with her mother while also looking at the reading book that contained the text. As with language acquisition, her mother had also spent many (more than 5) years generally unsuccessfully teaching her reading. After the type of MST interactions described above she mastered her *Peter and Jane* series, reading from Level 2 to Level 7.

Eye Contact

Maintaining eye contact is an important function for socialization and learning. In the treatment setting, Amy was introduced to the rules for talking to people, and how important it is for her eyes to be looking at peoples' faces. Then the following script was constructed, and repeated a number of times (again with variations in content and cadence, to keep it interesting for her, and "fresh"):

When you talk to people, can you look at your feet? No, when you talk to people, you cannot look at your feet. You must look at their face. Feet are not on the face.
  When you talk to people, can you look at their body? No, when you talk to people, you cannot look at their body. You must look at their face. Body is not on the face.
  When you talk to people, can you look at their nose? [this interaction goes on in the same way with the identification of other parts of the body]

The monologue was digitally recorded, and she listened to it many times. In subsequent interactions, if she looked away while talking, the therapist would recite some of the scripts above and she would listen. Very often she would establish eye contact immediately after listening to the scripted dialogue.

This illustrates the use of MST to address behavioral functions, many of which are difficult to change in therapy, and are considered among the more intractable aspects of "autistic syndrome" characteristics. In Amy's case, everyone around her began to observe, and many commented that "when she looks at things, you can see that she is looking at things meaningfully," "she doesn't gaze blankly anymore." She also began to spontaneously maintain eye contact with the person she was talking to or who was talking to her.

Learning the Abstract Concepts of Time

Given that a major thrust of the work with Amy was to build cognitive functions that would support enhanced learning, her therapist conducted an experiment using MST-oriented techniques to teach concepts of time that had proved very difficult for her to learn. Given her autistic behavior, age, and developmental level, the underlying mathematical concepts were presumed to be either absent or very fragile.

The therapist started reading and verbalizing the characteristics of an analog clock that she and Amy were both looking at, using both verbal and gestural communication. For example, when the clock showed 8:00:

Is the clock showing 9 o'clock? No, the clock is not showing 9 o'clock. The clock is showing 8:00.

Is the clock showing 8:30? No, the clock is not showing 8:30. The clock is showing 8:00.

Is the clock showing 8:00? Yes, the clock is showing 8:00.

Is the short hand pointing at number 6 on the clock? No, the short hand is not pointing to number 6 on the clock. The short hand is pointing to number 8 on the clock.

Is the short hand pointing at number 8 on the clock? Yes, the short hand is pointing at number 8 on the clock.

Is the long hand pointing at number 6 on the clock? [again, this dialogue was repeated, with variations a number of times, while continuing to look at the clock and direct Amy's attention to its features—primarily the location of the hands as they pointed to numbers]

The script was recorded and it was played for her many times by her mother and family, as she was looking at the clock. When it was determined that she was ready to understand the concept of "time span," using the passage of time on the hands of the clock—that is, to visualize the clock and count the time—the dialogue was changed, a small sample of which we present here:

> *Start at 8:30 a.m. and end at 9:15 a.m., is it 20 minutes? No, when we start at 8:30 a.m. and end at 9:15 it is not 20 minutes, it is 45 minutes.*
>   *If we start at 8:30 a.m. and end at 9:15 a.m., is it 1 hour? No, to start at 8:30 a.m. and end at 9:15 a.m. is not 1 hour, it is 45 minutes. If we start at 8:30 a.m. and end at 9:15 a.m., is it 45 minutes? Yes, to start at 8:30 a.m. is 45 minutes.*

This script was recorded and Amy repeatedly listened to it. The repetitive language in the script is due to the goal of building and assimilating a language structure to support time concepts, as well as to create flexibility in thinking. After several examples of time span, she began to count the time independently. When the question was changed to, *start at 5:30 p.m. and 30 minutes later, what is the time?* she paused for several minutes and answered *6:00 p.m.* Her answer indicated that she understood the concept of time span, as she hadn't been taught how to solve the new question. Amy was then presented with variations on the problem, using changed language. For example:

> *Daddy gets up at 6:30 a.m. He went into the bathroom and finished showering at 7:05 a.m. How much time did it take for him to shower?*

This introduced the concept of "starting time" and "ending time." The MST language was varied:

> *Daddy gets up at 6:30 a.m. He went into the bathroom and finished showering at 7:00 a.m. Is 6:30 a.m. the start time? Yes, 6:30 a.m. is the start time.*

This aspect of the case shows how MST can be used to support academic content and concept development, and that Amy had some latent mathematical concepts available to her.

Imitation

Amy had difficulty imitating. After MST, she could spontaneously imitate the adult's facial expression, gestures, actions, etc. She could not imitate a squatting posture. Her mother had tried to teach her for years.

Her body was quite hypotonic. Initially, someone would have to push her down and pull her up for her to achieve the squatting position. After repeated exposure to the MST scripted dialogue, she began to imitate squatting, in response to observing others and being exposed to verbal accompaniment. She responded to verbal encouragement (her parents had linked the need to learn to squat to a proposed trip to Australia) and answered, *All right, all right, I will squat. I want to go Australia.* Soon it was not necessary to help her physically; she did it solely in response to the verbal cueing. Here we show a small portion of a much longer MST script for this intervention:

> *Can you put both hands on the floor when you squat? No, you cannot put both your hands on the floor when you squat. Hands must be on the knees when you squat.*
>
> *Can you hold onto mummy when you squat? No, you cannot hold onto mummy when you squat. Hands must be on the knees when you squat.*
>
> *Must your hands be on the knees when you squat? Yes, hands must be on the knees when you squat.*
>
> *Can you tiptoe when you squat? No, you cannot tiptoe when you squat? Heels must touch the floor.*
>
> *Can you go to Australia if you cannot squat? No, you cannot go to Australia if you cannot learn to squat.*

The MST described here, developed in an innovative manner, appeared to help Amy reduce her autistic symptoms significantly. Her therapists described her as "more and more able to learn directly from her environment and become more and more so-called 'normal.'" Her parents, both of whom are medical doctors, took very careful notes to help describe her progress, and modify the treatment planning. Here are two particularly poignant examples:

> When her father saw her sitting in the room holding melted chocolate in her hand (she had taken it from the refrigerator)—she is forbidden to eat chocolate because of potential hyperactive behavior when she eats it, she giggled and told her father, *this chocolate is not nice.*

> At another time, when she saw her mother's wet eyes (her mother cried in the treatment room while observing Amy's newly acquired positive responses) Amy stopped, left the room, walked over to her mother, hugged her and said, *Mama, you are sad.* And she also copied her mother's facial expression, looking sad.

While one might question the accuracy of the initial diagnosis, the MST intervention clearly changed Amy's behavior. This case illustrates the role of language (and focusing, repetition, human engagement, etc.) in producing the change.

Case 3: Sam—
Language Delay

Sam was a 9-year-old boy with whom MST was used at the outset of treatment. His language was very limited: non-relevant speech, inability to speak in full and correct sentences, no spontaneous speech. He also showed aggressive behavior in school that generated at least one complaint by the teachers each week.

His situation was summarized as follows, after observation and a dynamic assessment using the Learning Propensity Assessment Device (LPAD) (Feuerstein, Feuerstein, Falik, & Rand, 2002): He was shown to possess good cognitive functions but was generally unable to express himself verbally.

We created a monologue consisting of simple sentences related to his reading book, and recorded them so that he could repeatedly listen to them at home while looking at the pictures in the book. This was done an average of 1 hour per day. For example: the MST developed for a sentence showing the character of Peter (after establishing that Peter was a human, a boy, was sitting on a park bench, etc.) in the book was:

Is a living thing here? Yes, a living thing is here because Peter is a living thing.

Is a person here? Yes, a person is here because Peter is a person.

Is a human here? Yes, a human is here because Peter is a human.

Is an animal here? No, an animal is not here because Peter is not an animal. Peter is a person.

[the picture showed other children playing in the background]

Is Peter in the same place as the other children? No, Peter is not in the same place as they are. Peter is here [pointing]. Here means the same place as he is in, not them.

Is Peter near them? No, Peter is not near them. Because he is here and they are not near him.

Is Peter close by? Yes, Peter is close by because here and close by are the same distance.

Is Jane here? No, Jane is not here because Peter is not Jane. Peter and Jane are two different persons.

Is a boy here? Yes, a boy is here because Peter is a boy.
Is a girl here? No, a girl is not here because Peter is not a girl. Peter and girl are of different genders. [this goes on to increase details, relate to other pictures in the book to differentiate and verbalize characteristics, and the like].

Notice how the soliloquy is related to concrete stimuli (the pictures) and to the action depicted in them. Notice also how the verbal interaction constructs syntax and presents both repetitions and variations. This is an excellent example of how the MST incorporates many of the structural elements (syntax, semantics, with implications for pragmatics) that we described in Chapter 4. The verbalizations also increase the conceptual abstraction of the experience, and introduce direction, distance, gender, and other differentiating concepts. Since it is a monologue, Sam is not asked to respond, simply to pay attention. His parents were instructed to hold him comfortably next to them, and not to be distracted or to terminate the exposure if he temporarily appeared not to be paying attention.

After a relatively short exposure time, Sam's parents observed a very significant change in speech. They reported that he was talking more spontaneously and remarking on objects and events in his environment. This was confirmed in subsequent treatment encounters. He began to try to talk more, even though his vocabulary was not strong. His parents were instructed to substitute or add words that appeared to be relevant to what he wanted to say. He was also reported to be much better behaved in school and at home, was less easily frustrated, and engaged in less acting out and distracting behavior. In school, his teachers reported that he was more responsive and was raising his hand to answer questions. Ultimately, our expectation is that monologues such as these, related both to concrete stimuli and interpersonal contacts, will stimulate further dialogue that the parents will be encouraged to engage in, and that they will, albeit slowly and gently.

Case 4: Damon—
An Angry Adolescent

Damon was an angry teenager who struggled with school. When faced with any situation that didn't fit his expectations, he would clam up and walk away. At home when frustrated he would threaten to run away and commit suicide.

Observation and assessment showed a lack of variation in his speech—always repeating similar sentences week after week, and from one situation to another. Moreover, he always appeared to be very angry. According to his mother, he was usually distant, very angry, and unhappy at home. His parents had to be very careful with what they said to him because if he didn't like what they said, he would leave the house or a setting (like a store) where the negative encounter occurred. His parents would have to look for him, find him, and bring him home.

MST for Damon was organized around the following activity: His therapists selected stimuli to present to him—a picture or a paragraph of factual content, usually containing a story with a clear theme presumed to be meaningful and evocative for him, based on their observations of his behavior—isolation, loneliness, anger, surprise. The goal was to elicit thoughts and language opportunities related to the themes, but not present them initially with any expectation or demand that he respond. After the therapist's soliloquy related to the picture or paragraph (that he looked at or read silently to himself), somewhat later, but not long after the initial exposure, Damon was encouraged to ask questions or make observations, and he would be gently responded to, and the soliloquy would be extended and embellished, usually by intensifying, explaining, or adding to the narrative. If he was unable to formulate responses, the therapists would return to the monologue format, and would ask and answer questions themselves (much as in the previous case illustrations) as he listened to the questions and answers.

After several months of exposure to the planned and repeated dialogue (using the MST format), Damon started to talk spontaneously whenever he came to the therapy sessions. His topics became more varied and he seldom repeated the same sentences or subjects. After almost 1 year of this exposure, with adaptations according to observations of his behavior and his responses, he showed himself to be inquisitive, interested, and engaged with the therapists. He began to ask about people, about the therapists' past experience, and the like. His mother said, "He is a happy boy at home now. He has started to show affection to his father [their relationship was very strained previously], even giving his father spontaneous hugs and kisses." He also became spontaneously affectionate with his mother. While this change in behavior is somewhat unusual for an adolescent, for Damon perhaps it represented a stage of attachment with his parents that he had not gone through and was now able to experience.

School behavior also improved. Teacher reports indicated that he began to make appropriate progress for his age and classroom expectations: He was described as being reliable and responsible, completing his homework, participating in class activities, and as being organized and using class time well, working both independently and in peer groups. It appears that using the MST approach in a situation such as this, in the context of a sensitive and responsive therapeutic milieu, may effect many changes that go beyond the initial treatment plan and intention. Here are some of the changes that Damon experienced.

When disagreeing with his mother about taking drama as another elective subject in school instead of another core subject, he was able to reason out that he had the choice to take the core subject in Year 9 or Year 10. He also told his mother, "You shouldn't have scolded me straight away when I told you. You should find out more first about this core subject." Previously, if he were in the same situation, he wouldn't have gotten the facts and reasoned it out with his mother, and likely would have left the scene with much anger.

Later he commented to his therapists: "I think I should report both of you to the Ministry of Education. What you all are teaching here is so different from other teachers. I must ask them to check you out. And tell them that both of you corrupt the students' parents. You all should stop corrupting our parents with rules" (all the while with a smile on his face and a feeling of connectedness). His comments and remarks are at the same level with his peers now. Previously, it was always the same stereotyped and repetitive speech, and devoid of humor, irony, and social nuance, all of which he is now able to demonstrate both in therapy, in his family, and in his larger environment. These anecdotes reflect his social awareness, connectedness to others, and a reflective awareness of his environment.

SUMMARY

The cases presented in this chapter illustrate the range of application of MST—the kinds of activities that comprise it, the types of individuals and learning/language/cognitive deficiencies that it benefits, and the ingenuity and flexibility that are required and possible in its application. At the Feuerstein Institute (in Jerusalem), in our various clinical programs, our therapists work with clients (those who have experienced brain injuries, children who function within the autistic spectrum, and others) to incorporate aspects of MST. As we indicated in the Preface, they have helped to formulate many of the specific suggestions that we have brought into this volume. Within the therapy sessions, and in consultation with parents and caretakers, we encourage the creation of a rich linguistic environment, and have many case examples of the application and effects of this approach on a variety of dimensions of functioning—cognitive, social, academic, etc. We are also extending the application of the method to the elderly, considering the enrichment of the language environment to have important effects on the course of mental deterioration so common in that population.

We emphasize that we are at the relative beginning of the implementation of the MST method. As we indicate in the next chapter, there is much that we have yet to learn. The theory is clear, the effects are powerful, and the underlying structural changes are starting to be understood. We know that there will be resistance to its application, as we have addressed in several places earlier in this book. It is our hope that the cases presented in this chapter will elucidate the concepts and encourage the reader to try, to explore, and to differentiate what can be done.

In our interactions with parents and teachers who have been helped by this method, and other applications of mediated learning experience, we are often told, "You have done a miracle, you have changed our child, and our lives!" To which we respond, "Yes it is a miracle that we all celebrate. But *it was not produced miraculously*. It was the product of hard work!" These cases illustrate that clearly.

CHAPTER 11

The Challenge and
the Promise of MST

There are many opportunities and challenges to consider in the application of MST. There is need for research into the approach and to further understand its potential for application. As we conclude this book, we will outline some of the issues and variables that we need to know more about to extend and support the method.

SOME EARLY RESULTS
AND QUESTIONS FOR THE FUTURE

When we have provided practitioners with an initial, experimental version of the method, and have presented it in lectures and seminars, great interest has been expressed and readiness and enthusiasm regarding implementing it have been generated. We have encouraged this interest, and many have tried it out. It has led to the gathering of preliminary results, and has generated a number of issues and variables that appear to be important to identify and study further.

The first result has been the universally positive reaction of those who have applied the method. Enthusiastic reports of positive outcomes, even with individuals who present long-standing and severe speech and language deficits, have been reported. From our point of view the positive effects appear so rapidly and with such strength as to belie the severity and extent of prior conditions. One reviewer of a manuscript based on MST submitted for publication in a professional journal remarked that the submitted outcomes of using the method seemed unlikely (in the scope and extent of the changes reported), with which we could not disagree, even though contrary to the reports we received. However, our experience and those of others lead us to expect and anticipate very positive results, given a systematic and well-designed application of the method (see cases in Chapter 10). We know that this must be subjected to controlled research so that we can identify the many variables that emerge from its use with children and others who can benefit from the stimulation and enrichment of their language experience.

We consider a particularly rich area for research investigation—related to the MST method—that of the mirroring functions in the brain, especially related to language acquisition and development, and the already well-investigated mechanisms of overheard language and the role of imitation. With regard to MST, we can ask what the effects of these processes are, and what kinds of roles they play in application. We believe that there is already a great deal of supportive research from the neurosciences that may offer explanatory or elaborative support for MST (see Chapter 3).

SUMMARIZING THE PROCESS AND PROSPECTS

We conclude this book by briefly reviewing some of our essential concepts in the development and provision of MST. The use of soliloquy—formulated systematically in the framework of mediated self-talk—has an important contribution to make as a modality for overcoming or remediating language delay, deficit, or loss. We have striven to present a description of language disorders to address these needs, largely through a perspective on positive models of language for the developing child and/or adult where appropriate development has not occurred or dysfunction is experienced. We have proposed activities for those with specific and clinical language delays and deficiencies, applying the method to overcome difficulties and build language competence. Consequently, we have emphasized the need to be very familiar with the structural and developmental aspects of language, so that mediation can present specific responses and activities reflective of them. It is for this reason that we provide the details of language structure and usage in Chapter 4, and many suggestions for responses keyed to elements of linguistic functions in Chapters 5 and 6.

The information in those chapters is sufficient for constructing effective soliloquies and engaging in MST, but is actually designed to be a guide to further activities and responses that parents, teachers, and others are encouraged to develop and practice. Many readers may wish to go further, however, to better understand the underlying structures and processes of language, and are strongly encouraged to do so, using the suggestions and references provided at various places in the book.

In Chapter 5, we introduced the importance of differentiating the environmental versus the therapeutic focus, and we want to summarize it here. MST has the potential to enlarge the activities of speech and language or other specialists, adding to their repertoires of tools when working with problems of autism, aphasia, brain injuries, developmental delays, and other language disorders, as well as in adults affected by various conditions impairing speech recognition, production, and ideation. However, soliloquy can also fill the gaps between the periods of therapeutic contact and the verbal/linguistic interactions with parents, teachers, caregivers, peers, and others in the life of the individual. The therapeutic focus may be strongly reinforced by the environmental, and both become important opportunities to enlarge the child's exposure to linguistic models in meaningful environments. The everyday and natural provision of MST reinforces the typically more limited (a few hours per week at the maximum, more often just 1 hour a week) therapeutic contacts that the child may have with speech and language therapists, play therapists, and in occupational or physical therapy. In this way, the communication experience is not limited to the specialist, but is an important part of the interactions of all who relate to children (and other language-disabled individuals), and can be an important support for the therapist (and their therapeutic interventions). Parental or other interactions may be directed by the therapist, collaboration and consultations may be constructed, bringing the therapeutic component into the life space of the child or adult in need. Such collaboration is both useful and necessary (see the cases presented in Chapter 10).

Through the mechanism of overheard language, which we described in an earlier chapter as the *pipeline through which the soliloquy impacts the listener*, the individual is increasingly exposed to the soliloquy. Eventually, if the MST has been effective, the interaction becomes more reciprocal, in physical attention and focusing, and in generating verbal responses.

The role of mediated learning experience (MLE) transforms MST from a simple exposure to language models into a focused and intentional interaction, with mediational components that can be adopted and used by parents, teachers, and others, as we described in Chapter 2, enriching the learner's experience with the linguistic and—even more importantly—cognitive elements of his or her world.

Throughout this book, we have identified and described the essential elements that must be focused on and presented in the structure of MST. To put it into effective action requires attention to four major operational strategies:

1. Creating lists of meaningful and relevant vocabulary words and language structures to systematically include in adult self-talk, and to listen for and find evidenced in the child's self-talk.
2. Analyzing the experiential and behavioral situations that the child experiences and that serve as the focus for strategically planned soliloquy.

3. Including gestural and other non-verbal components, as a way to visualize the movements, objects, and enunciated aspects of the spoken word(s). This offers a demonstration of the action of the object and mimicry of the action and affect, serving to "punctuate" the intensity, structure of meaning, and experience of the verbal mode of speech.
4. Infusing MLE into the interactions, enlarging the world of content for the child, presenting experiences not otherwise available or attended to in the child's direct experience. This enhances the propensity for abstract thinking, moving away from dependence on and the limitations of direct exposure, and enabling representation of both experiences and ideas.

SUMMING UP

Even if the child does not appear ready, MST presented with the provision of MLE becomes a rich source of exposure, *going beyond where the child is and moving toward what the learner can become.* In this sense, the *mediation* of MST involves considerably more than a focused differentiation of certain targeted aspects of the speech process. It has the potential to consolidate or improve articulatory difficulties or other deficiencies specifically present in the speech repertoire of the individual—as long as it is applied using the structural and implementational elements that we have described in earlier chapters.

The role of soliloquy, especially at the preschool level, is not only to encourage children to speak, but also to offer models of linguistic formulations, learning how to describe experiences, access memories of past experiences, and plan for the future. MST may also be used in the classroom with children experiencing learning or verbal language deficits, where the teacher or teaching assistant can work with the child to encourage motor and other learning activities accompanied by soliloquy.

Usually teachers are taught to use only the language the children have and bring to the classroom environment, and not to go beyond where the child is. The focus of this book, conversely, is to go beyond. We have used the phrase "enriching the child's linguistic environment" throughout this book with just this point in mind.

To a certain extent, the establishment of the soliloquy activity on the part of the parents, siblings, teachers, or other agents, or generated by the child's spontaneous self-talk, creates a speaking environment in which the non-speaking child, or the limited-speaking child or individual, is immersed. It matters less—and in fact should be a clear part of the mediator's intentionality—that the individual can or cannot respond to it (in a real-time context). We must continuously remind ourselves that *soliloquy is not contingent on the child's capacity to respond!*

The authors are encouraged that without exception, those who have been oriented to early experimental versions of the MST method report consistent, strong, and relatively rapid improvements in the language functioning of the children to whom it is applied. Importantly, such results have occurred even with children who present relatively severe special needs and have been non-verbal well into their latency years, contrary to earlier conceptions of a critical period for the development of language function. These outcomes occur more rapidly and more intensely than we initially anticipated or even predicted. Moreover, the optimism and enthusiasm expressed by those who are starting to use MST is encouraging, and encourages us to think further and to explore and experiment with its practical applications and clinical potential (as the cases in Chapter 10 illustrate).

Millions of children come to the classroom without the language to ensure their success. This was the senior author's (Professor Feuerstein) early motivation to develop this approach. It has led to years of development, practice, modification, and reformulation. If we can meet the needs of these learners, we will have done much to improve the quality of their lives and their communities. And to do so by involving parents, teachers, and professionals in positive and sustaining interactions is truly the *challenge and the promise!*

The Need for Systematic Experimental Studies

We know that research is required to go deeper into the conditions and variables suggested by initial experiences. We must identify the relevant and critical variables present in the approach—looking carefully for the conditions that should be present and controlled in its application, elaborating our state of knowledge and addressing the ultimate efficacy of the approach.

What is required is the formulation and testing of hypotheses regarding what works, why it works, under what conditions it works, and other dimensions of implementation—differential applications, with differing populations and syndromes, issues of "dosage" (intensity of provision, range of application, types and extent of repetition, etc.), sequences of functions, and the like. The application of MST offers many interesting and important opportunities for investigation.

Some Potential Outcomes That Extend Our Knowledge

At the outset, our perspectives on MST are framed by a number of concerns—theoretical constructs (what is hypothesized to occur; predicted outcomes or contributory factors based on other bases of knowledge); clarifying the focus on the developmental and structural nature of linguistic processes; systematic observations of behavior and functioning, related to populations that are selected for study; identifying needs and belief systems—identifying what is important as an object of focus and what are the hierarchies of needs; logistics of populations and settings—what is possible, needed, worthy of spotlighting. The ultimate effectiveness of MST rests on all of these potential variables. We can, however, estimate some of the relevant and elucidating aspects of the process of designing a research agenda for this method. The overall goal, however, is to create well thought out, controlled, and systematic investigations based on meaningful "researchable questions." And, of course, in the nature of research, the pursuit of these questions will lead to the generation of other variables that were not immediately apparent.

Some Specific Research Questions

What are the specific aspects of MLE that contribute to the effectiveness of the soliloquy? We believe that isolating the effects of the mediational component will offer important cues to the effectiveness of the method, and offer information on general aspects of stimulating language development and overcoming linguistic deficits.

What is the relevance, sequence, and best way to present the language structures that underlie the approach? With regard to the linkage of soliloquy to general conceptions of the development of language, the question can be asked about whether this structure is relevant, helpful, in the proper sequence, defined appropriately, and the like.

If MST is successful, and as the child begins to respond to the mediation, what reactions of the learner and what further aspects of the linguistic interaction need to be constructed and conveyed? What are they, how should they be constructed, what are the best mechanisms for conveyance, and what are the outcomes? This is an area of important extension of MST

How does neural plasticity relate to language development and the modifiability of cognitive functions? The evidence is strong and persuasive, but is still relatively new and undifferentiated. MST offers rich opportunities to explore a variety of neural and behavioral dimensions of the relationship, identifying, manipulating, and observing effects, and using advanced technologies and models.

What is the role of language development on behavioral and social attunement? Researching MST on dimensions such as these can contribute to the development of the neurosciences. This is particularly relevant as an opportunity to move neuroscientific studies increasingly toward models involving human factors. It seems to us that questions like this have great potential for the perspective of the linguistic and behavioral experience that MST offers.

How should we train and support those who are learning and applying MST? Lastly, what are the essential elements and experiences that need to be structured into training and support to make MST work and be sustained? Our preliminary experience points to a number of variables—types of knowledge to be acquired, ways to convey it, identifying and observing needs and skills of the provider, needs and developmental potential in the learner, etc. For example, how do we present a stable and continuous orientation to the desired models for training and support so that soliloquy will be effective and sustained, and how do we help the producer of the MST to be aware of the changes imposed on the learner and how those changes are responded to?

References

Au, T. K-F., Knightly, L. M., Jun, S-A., & Oh, J. S. (2002). Overhearing a language during childhood. *Psychological Science, 13,* 238–243.

Baldwin, J. M. (1885). *Mental development in the child and the race.* New York: Macmillan.

Bates, E., Elman, J., Johnson, M., Karmiloff-Smith, A., Parisi, D., & Plunkett, K. (1998). Innateness and emergentism. In W. Bechtel & G. Graham (Eds.), *A companion to cognitive science* (pp. 2–10.). Oxford: Basil Blackwell.

Bernstein, B. (1959). Public language: Some sociological implications of a linguistic form. *British Journal of Sociology, 10,* 311–326.

Bernstein, D. K., & Tiegerman-Farber, E. (1997). *Language and communication disorders in children.* Needham Heights, MA: Allyn and Bacon.

Bloom, L., Hood, L., & Lichtbown, P. (1974). Imitation in language: If, when, and why. *Cognitive Psychology, 6,* 380–420.

Buccino, G., Lui, F., Canessa, N., Patteri, I., Lagravinese, G., et al. (2004). Neural circuits involved in the recognition of actions performed by non-conspecifics: An fMRI study. *Journal of Cognitive Neuroscience, 16,* 1–14.

Carr, L., Iacoboni, M., Dubeau, M. C., Mazziotta, J. C., & Lenzi, G. L. (2002). Neural mechanisms of empathy in humans: A relay from neural systems for imitation to limbic areas. *Proceedings of the National Academy of Science, USA, 100,* 5497–5502.

Crain, S., & Lillo Martin, D. (1997). *Linguistic theory and language acquisition.* Oxford: Blackwell.

Crossley, R. (1997). *Speechless: Facilitating communication for people without voices.* New York: Dutton.

Davydov, V. V. (1988). The category of activity and mental reflection in the theory of A. N. Leont'ev. *Journal of Russian and East European Psychology, 19*(4), 3–39.

Decety, J., & Chaminade, T. (2003). When the self represents the other: A new cognitive neuroscience view on psychological identification. *Consciousness and Cognition, 12,* 577–596.

Diaz, R. M., & Berk, L. E. (Eds.). (1992). *Private speech: From social interaction to self-regulation.* Hillsdale, NJ: Erlbaum.

Diaz, R. M., Neal, C. J., & Amaya-Williams, M. (1992). The social origins of self-regulation. In L. C. Moll (Ed.), *Vygotsky and education: Instructional implications and applications of sociohistorical psychology* (pp. 127–154). New York: Cambridge University Press.

Diaz, R. M., Winsler, A., Atencio, D. J., & Harbers, K. (1992). Mediation of self-regulation through the use of private speech. *International Journal of Cognitive Education and Mediated Learning, 2,* 155–167.

Doidge, N. (2007). *The brain that changes itself.* New York: Viking.

Fernald, A., & Kuhl, P. (1987). Acoustic determinants for motherese speech. *Infant Behavior Development, 10,* 279–293.

Feuerstein, R. (1979). Ontogeny of learning in man. In M. A. B. Brazier (Ed.), *Brain mechanisms in memory and learning: From the single neuron to man.* New York: Raven Press.

Feuerstein, R., Falik, L. H., & Bohács, K. (2010). A kozvetitett szolilokvia: A nyelv es a kommunikacio mediacioja a belso beszeden keresztul (Mediated soliloquy: Mediation of language and communication through self-talk). Magyar Pedagogia, 110(2), 97–118.

Feuerstein, R., Feuerstein, R. S., Falik, L. H., & Rand, Y. (2002). *The dynamic assessment of cognitive modifiability: The learning propensity assessment device: Theory, instruments, and techniques.* Jerusalem, Israel: ICELP Press.

Feuerstein, R., Feuerstein, R. S., Falik, L. H., & Rand, Y. (2006). *Creating and enhancing cognitive modifiability: The Feuerstein instrumental enrichment program.* Jerusalem, Israel: ICELP Press.

Feuerstein, R., & Hoffman, M. (1994). *Instrumental enrichment teacher's guides* [14 instruments]. Arlington, Heights, IL: IRI Skylight.

Feuerstein, R., & Lewin-Benham, A. (2012). *What learning looks like: Mediated learning in theory and practice, K–6.* New York: Teachers College Press.

Feuerstein, R., Mintzker, Y., & Feuerstein, R. S. (2006). *Mediated learning experience: Guidelines for parents.* Jerusalem, Israel: ICELP Press.

Fogassi, L., & Ferrari, P. F. (2007). Mirror neurons and the evolution of embedded language. *Current Directions in Psychology Science, 16*(3), 136–141.

Gallese, V. (2009). Mirror neurons, embodied simulation, and the neural basis of social identification. *Psychoanalytic Dialogues, 19,* 519–536.

Gallese, V., Keysers, C., & Rizzolatti, G. (2004) A unifying view of the basis of social cognition. *Trends in Cognitive Sciences, 8,* 396–403.

Goleman, D. (2006). *Social intelligence.* New York: Bantam Books.

Iacoboni, M. (2005). Neural mechanisms of imitation. *Current Opinion in Neurobiology, 15,* 632–637.

Iacoboni, M., Woods, R. P., Brass, M., Bekkering, M., Mazziotta, J. C., & Rizzolatti, G. (1999). Cortical mechanisms of human imitation. *Science, 286,* 2526–2528.

Indefrey, P., & Levelt, W. J. M. (2004). The spatial and temporal signatures of word production components. *Cognition, 92,* 101–144.

Kleim, J. A., & Jones, T. A. (2008). Principles of experience-dependent neural plasticity: Implications for rehabilitation after brain damage. *Supplement: Journal of Speech, Language, and Hearing Research, 51*, 5225–5231.

Kohler, L., Keysers, C., Umilta, M. A., Fogassi, L., Gallese, V., & Rizzolatti, G. (2002). Hearing sounds, understanding actions: Action representation in mirror neurons. *Science, 297*, 846–848.

Kuhl, P. K. (2004). Early language acquisition: Cracking the speech code. *Nature Reviews/Neuroscience, 5*, 831–843.

Kuhl, P. K., & Melzhoff, A. N. (1982). The bimodal perception of speech in infancy. *Science, 218*, 1138–1141.

Kuhl, P. K., & Melzhoff, A. N. (1996). Infant vocalizations in response to speech: Vocal imitation and developmental change. *Journal of the Acoustical Society of America, 100*, 2425–2438.

Landauer, T. K., & Dumais, S. T. (1997). A solution to Plato's problem: The latent semantic analysis theory of acquisition. *Psychological Review, 104*, 211–240.

Liberman, A. M., & Mattingly, I. G. (1985). The motor theory of speech perception revised. *Cognition, 21*, 1–36.

Lieven, E. (1994). Crosslinguistic and crosscultural aspects of language addressed to children. In C. Gallaway & B. Richers (Eds.), *Input and interaction in language acquisition* (pp. 56–73). Cambridge, England: Cambridge University Press.

Masur, E. F. (1995). Infants' early verbal imitation and their later lexical development. *Merrill-Palmer Quarterly, 41*, 286–306.

Masur, E. F. (1997). Maternal labeling of novel and familiar objects: Implications for children's development of lexical constructs. *Journal of Child Language, 24*, 427–439.

Melzhoff, A. N. (2007). "Like me": A foundation for social cognition. *Developmental Science, 10*, 126–134.

Mesister, I. G., Boroojerdi, B., Foltys, H., Sparing, R., Huber, W., & Topper, R. (2002). Motor cortex hand area and speech: Implications for the development of language. *Neuropyschologia, 41*, 401–406.

Miller, G. A. (1977). *Spontaneous apprentices: Children and language*. New York: Seabury Press.

O'Grady, W. (2008). Innateness, universal grammar, and emergentism. *Lingua, 118*(4), 620–631.

Ohima-Tekama, Y., Goodz, E., & Deverensky, J. (2008). Birth order effects on early language development: Do second-born children learn from overheard speech? *Child Development, 67*(2), 621–634.

Piaget, J. (1977). *The essential Piaget*. New York: Basic Books.

Piaget, J., & Inhelder, B. (1969). *The psychology of the child*. New York: Basic Books.

Rizzolatti, G., & Arbib, M. A. (1998). Language within our grasp. *TINS, 21*(5), 188–194.

Rizzolatti, G., & Craighero, L. (2004). The mirror neuron system. *Annual Review of Neurosciences, 27,* 169–192.

Saffran, J. R., Aslin, R. N., & Newport, E. L. (1996). Statistical learning by 8 month old infants. *Science, 274,* 321–324.

Schubotz, R. I., & Von Cramen, D. Y. (2001). Functional organization of the lateral premotor cortex: fMRI reveals different regions activated by anticipation of object properties, location and speed. *Cognitive Brain Research, 11*(1), 97–112.

Seyal, M., Mull, B., Bhullar, N., Ahmad, T., & Gage, B. (1999). Anticipation and execution of a sample reading task enhance corticospinal excitability. *Clinical Neuropsysiology, 110,* 424–429.

Siegel, D. (2007). *The mindful brain.* New York: W.W. Norton.

Siegel, D. J. (2010). *Mindsight.* New York: Bantam.

Singer, T. (2006). The neuronal basis and ontogeny of empathy and mind reading: Review of literature and implications for further research. *Neuroscience and Biobehavioral Reviews, 6,* 855–863.

Skoyles, J. R. (1997). Speech phones are a replication code. *Medical Hypothesis, 50,* 167–173.

Skoyles, J. R. (2008). *Mirror neurons and the motor theory of speech.* Available at http://www.citeulike.org/user/ly3/article/862620

Skoyles, J. R. (2010). Mapping of heard speech into articulation information and speech acquisition. *Proceedings of the National Academy of Sciences, 107,* 18.

Umilta, M. A., Kohler, E., Gallese, V., Fogassi, L., Fadiga, L., et al. (2001). "I know what you are doing": A neurophysiological study. *Neuron, 32,* 91–101.

Vygotsky. L. S. (1987). Thinking and speech. In R. W. Rieber, A. S. Carton (Eds.) & N. Minick (Trans.), *The collected works of L. S. Vygotsky: Vol. 1., Problems of general psychology* (pp. 37–85). New York: Plenum.

Wicker, B., Keysers, C., Plaillyu, J., Royet, J. P., Gallese, V., & Rizzolatti, G. (2002). Both of us disgusted my insula: The common neural basis of seeing and feeling disgust. *Neuron, 40,* 655–664.

Zazzo, R. (1962). *Conduites de Conscience.* Neuchatel: Delachaux et Niestle.

Index

Motherese, 5–7
  babbling and, 40–41
  defined, 5
  in language acquisition and
      development, 5–7, 17
  MST compared with, 5–7
Motor vocalization, 42
MST. *See* Mediated self-talk (MST)
Mull, B., 31
Multi-sensory stimulation effect, 27
Mutism, selective, 90

Naming of objects, 52, 72–73
Neal, C. J., 8–9
Neural plasticity
  critical elements in promoting,
      25–27
  in language development, 130
  mirror neurons and, 24–25, 28–33
  overhearing and, 7
Neural resonance circuits, 24
Neurophysiology, 24–33
  activity theory and, 28
  animal research in, 31, 57
  basis for speech acquisition in, 16
  human research in, 32, 33
  imitation and, 29–30
  intentionality/reciprocity in, 31–33
  mirror neurons in imitation process,
      8, 15, 24, 76
  mirror neurons in language
      acquisition and development,
      8, 15, 24–25, 28–33, 76
  MST and, 2–3, 24, 27
  neuroimaging techniques in, 24–25,
      29, 30, 31–32
Newport, E. L., 45
Nonverbal communication
  facial expression, 35–36
  gestures, 56, 76, 78, 108, 109
  imitation of, 22–23, 78
Nouns, 44, 54, 109–110
Novelty effect, 26

Objects, as referents to action, 54

Observation
  comparative, 79, 82–83
  observational monologues with
      early intervention (case),
      107–112
O'Grady, W., 45
Oh, J. S., 7
Ohima-Tekama, Y., 7
Open-ended questions, 54
Optimal timing potential effect, 26
Orofacial myofunctional disorders,
    90
Overhearing. *See also* Imitation
  in language acquisition and
      development, 2, 3, 6, 7, 9–10,
      59–60, 67–68, 108, 125
  motherese and, 6
  nature of, 3, 7, 59–60, 67–68

Paralinguistic elements, of MST, 5,
    35–36
Parisi, D., 45
Parts of speech, 44–45
Patteri, I., 32
Persistence effect, 26
Personalization, 53, 75
Phonetic awareness, 40–41
Phonology
  disorders of, 92
  nature of, 40–41, 46–49, 91
Piaget, J., 8, 13, 22, 28
Planned application of MST, 63–64
Pliallyu, J., 33
Plunkett, K., 45
Poverty of repertoire
  disorders of, 93
  nature of, 12, 91
Pragmatics
  disorders of, 92
  nature of, 45–50, 91
Prefrontal cortex, 27
Prelinguistic elements of language,
    35–36
  in Down syndrome case, 96–97
Prepositions, 112–113

About the Authors

Professor Reuven Feuerstein formulated the theory of structural cognitive modifiability (SCM) and mediated learning experience (MLE) in the 1950s, as a response to the need to save the children who survived the Holocaust. Professor L. J. Cronbach said his work has "changed the face of modern psychology." Professor Feuerstein founded the Hadassah-WIZO-Canada Research Institute, which became the International Center for the Enhancement of Learning Potential (ICELP), and is now the Feuerstein Institute. He has fostered the development of programs for the assessment and intervention of learning and development, based on his theories, that have generated a new field of application—dynamic assessment and the improvement of cognitive functioning. These programs have been disseminated throughout the world, and have been translated into more than 17 languages. He continues to develop his concepts, to stimulate scholars and practitioners from all corners of the world, and to see and help children and families.

Professor Louis H. Falik is emeritus professor of counseling at San Francisco State University in the United States and a senior scholar focusing on training, research, and professional development at the international Feuerstein Institute (formerly the International Center for the Enhancement of Modifiability—ICELP) in Jerusalem, Israel. He has trained and collaborated since 1985 with Professor Reuven Feuerstein in the development and dissemination of his theories on cognitive modifiability and practical implementations. He is author and co-author of a number of books and research papers on dynamic assessment (LPAD), the Feuerstein Instrumental Enrichment (FIE) program, and mediated learning experience (MLE). He is a clinical and educational psychologist with extensive experience in the training and application of FIE and the LPAD in child, adolescent, and adult populations, focusing on both learning disabilities and academic performance and enhancement objectives.

Rabbi Refael S. Feuerstein is deputy chairman of the Feuerstein Institute (formerly ICELP) in Jerusalem, Israel. He has furthered the work of Professor Reuven Feuerstein by extending the theoretical and practical applications of programs to materialize structural cognitive modifiability, bringing the practical benefits of this theory to an increasingly diverse range of populations and applications. As Deputy Chairman, he assists Professor Feuerstein in furthering the conceptual and operational development of cognitive modifiability and mediated learning experience, and coordinates professional development activities within Israel and internationally. He is also the primary developer of the Instrumental Enrichment—Basic and Learning Propensity Device—basic programs that are applied to young children and severely low functioning older learners.

Krisztina Bohács is a lecturer and guest teacher at Eötvös Loránd University, Budapest. She is earning her Ph.D. at the University of Szeged in Educational Sciences. Her special interest is the relationship of cognition and language development in the family context. She is the professional head of the Foundation for Mediated Learning, a clinical center in Budapest that has treated children with all kinds of learning disabilities using Professor Feuerstein's theory and applied systems with great success. With her colleagues she is participating in international research projects (such as the Daffodil Project). She is highly experienced in giving courses in MLE for parents of children with learning or developmental difficulties, and she is also involved in in-service teacher training.